About the Author

Richard Webster (New Zealand) travels around the world lecturing and conducting workshops on psychic subjects. He is the author of over twenty-five books, including *Spirit Guides & Angel Guardians*, *Feng Shui for Beginners*, and the forthcoming *Candle Magic for Beginners*.

Miracles
Inviting the Extraordinary Into Your Life

Richard Webster

2004
Llewellyn Publications
St. Paul, Minnesota 55164-0383, U.S.A.

First Edition
First Printing, 2004

Book design and editing by Michael Maupin
Cover design by Gavin Dayton Duffy

Library of Congress Cataloging-in-Publication Data
Webster, Richard, 1946–
    Miracles : inviting the extraordinary into your life / Richard Webster.
      p. cm.
    Includes bibliographical references and index.
    ISBN 0-7387-0606-X
    1. Miracles. I. Title.

BL487.W43 2004
202'.117—dc22   2004046469

Llewellyn Publications
A Division of Llewellyn Worldwide, Ltd.
P.O. Box 64383, Dept. 0-7387-0606-X
St. Paul, MN 55164-0383, U.S.A.
www.llewellyn.com

Printed in the United States of America

Other Books by Richard Webster

Forthcoming

For my younger son,
Philip

Contents

Introduction

WHEN MY GRANDDAUGHTER was four-years-old, she and I spent a wonderful afternoon watching a monarch butterfly emerge from its chrysalis, exercise its wings, and finally fly away.

"That's a miracle!" Eden exclaimed.

I was impressed that she seemed to know what a miracle was. To her young eyes, the appearance of a beautiful butterfly, that had been a caterpillar just a week or two earlier, was a miracle. It made me think of Walt Whitman's poem "Miracles":

> Why, who makes much of a miracle?
> As to me I know of nothing else but miracles . . .
> . . . To me every hour of the light and dark is a miracle,
> Every cubic inch of space is a miracle,
> Every square yard of the surface of the earth is spread
> with the same,
> Every foot of the interior swarms with the same.
> To me the sea is a continual miracle,

The fishes that swim—the rocks—the motion of the
waves—the ships with men in them,
What stranger miracles are there?

To Whitman, everything was a miracle, and all of his poems reflect that conviction. In one sense everything is a miracle, but a real miracle needs more than this. We know that the morning comes after the night. To Walt Whitman, this fact is a miracle, but because it happens every day, without fail, we take it for granted. Walt Whitman's miracles are wonders, but are they *true* miracles?

Saint Augustine would have partially agreed with Walt Whitman as he believed that "all natural things are filled with the miraculous."[1] However, he also believed that the creation of the world out of nothing in just six days was the only true miracle. Life itself, could also be considered the only miracle. Many scientists today are trying to discover the secrets behind the miracle of life.

The standard definition of a true miracle is something that goes against the normal laws of nature and is usually ascribed to some supernatural power. In fact, virtually all religions express a belief in miracles. St. Thomas Aquinas (c. 1225–1274) believed that a miracle had to be beyond the natural power of any created person or thing to produce. As humans were created, this meant that only God could work miracles.[2] However, other religious authorities have put forward different views. Pope Benedict XIV (1675–1758) wrote that a miracle is something that is beyond "the power of visible and corporeal nature only."[3] This means that angels could work miracles, as could people if they were temporarily granted powers that were normally beyond them. An example of the latter occurred when the Apostle Peter healed a man who had been lame since birth (Acts 3: 1–9).

It is understandable that the Christian church wanted all miracles to be ascribed to God, as they could then use them as evidence of God's existence. However, the Bible contains a number of instances of miracles, such as Peter's healing of the lame man, that were performed by people. Naturally, they were performing these healings in God's name.

A better definition was offered by the twentieth century Protestant theologian Paul Tillich (1886–1965), who wrote:

> A genuine miracle is first of all an event which is astonishing, unusual, shaking, without contradicting the rational structure of reality. In the second place it is an event which points to the mystery of being, expressing its relation to us in a definite way. In the third place it is an occurrence which is received as a sign-event in an ecstatic experience. Only if these conditions are fulfilled can one speak of a genuine miracle.[4]

Scottish philosopher and skeptic David Hume (1711–1776) believed that "a miracle may be accurately defined as a transgression of a law of nature by a particular volition of the Deity, or by the interposition of some invisible agent."[5]

In his book *The Concept of Miracle*, Richard Swinburne defined a miracle as "an event of an extraordinary kind, brought about by a god, and of religious significance."[6]

C. S. Lewis (1898–1963), the twentieth-century academic and Christian apologist, defined a miracle as being "an interference with Nature by supernatural power."[7] Lewis deliberately created this "popular" definition as he felt that it would be more relevant to the average person than a more theological definition.

Many people today would eliminate any mention of the divine, and define a miracle as being an extraordinary coincidence. This can create problems, as Professor R. F. Holland suggested in a paper he wrote for *American Philosophical Quarterly* in 1965, called "The Miraculous." He related a story about a small boy who was riding a toy car near a railway crossing. A wheel of his car gets trapped down the side of one of the lines just as an express train is due. A curve in the track would prevent the driver of the train from seeing the child until it was too late. The boy's mother comes running out of her house to look for her son just as the train appeared. Amazingly, the train stops just a few feet from the child. The mother thanks God for a miracle, but in reality the train driver had not seen the boy. He had fainted, and the brakes came on automatically when he ceased applying pressure to the control lever.[8] Was this a miracle, a coincidence, good luck, or the grace of God? I would define it as a miracle, because, if the train driver had not fainted, or had fainted a second or two later, the boy would have died. Other people might describe it as an extraordinary coincidence, or maybe a miraculous coincidence. Christians might say it was the grace of God, while others might say it was the child's karma or fate. As I believe it to be a miracle, I also believe that miracles can occur to people of all faiths, as well as to people with none.

Reverend Johannes Osiander (1657–1724) was someone whose tale appeared to be one miracle after another. On one occasion a wild boar charged him and knocked him down, but he was uninjured. His horse fell over during a flood, and the reverend was trapped underneath. Again, he received no injuries whatsoever. Bandits fired a fusillade of gunfire at him, but missed. He was buried by an avalanche, and climbed out unscathed. A blizzard blew him into the icy River Rhine. He swam to shore, and did not even catch a cold. A tree fell on him. Of course, the Reverend Johannes crawled out from under it unharmed. When he ventured to sea, he survived a shipwreck. The boat that came to rescue him ran right over him, but naturally, the Reverend Johannes was not hurt.[9] Most people would consider surviving any one of these instances to be a miracle.

Of course, in daily life we frequently use the word "miracle" in the sense that Walt Whitman did. Someone who performs a magnificent feat might be termed "a miracle man." A doctor who cures someone who was thought to be terminally ill might be called "a miracle worker." In his diary, John Evelyn mentioned "that miracle of a youth, Mr. Christopher Wren."[10] Sir Philip Sidney, the Elizabethan poet-soldier, received a similar compliment. Richard Carew, a fellow poet, wrote, "Will you have all in all for prose and verse? Take the miracle of our age, Sir Philip Sidney."[11] Unfortunately, Sir Philip Sidney died twenty-eight years before this accolade appeared. Samuel Taylor Coleridge, in his poem "Kubla Khan," wrote, "it was a miracle of rare device/A sunny pleasure-dome with caves of ice."

A few weeks ago I sent a parcel to a friend in England. The post office delivered it in just three days, and my friend described this as "miraculous." It was wonderful service, but could it honestly be described as a miracle? Not long ago I was reading the sporting section of my local newspaper and saw the headline "Miracle Win." Although the weaker team had managed to win this particular game, the achievement was obviously far from being a miracle. A few months ago we arranged to meet friends to see a movie, and they arrived just as the film started. They told us that the traffic had been so bad that it was a miracle they got to the cinema at all.

The word "miracle" has come a long way from its original meaning, derived from the Latin *miraculum*, which means "to cause wonder and astonishment," and *mirus*, which means "wonderful to see." A miracle, therefore, is something that is extraordinary, inexplicable, and unexplainable by normal standards. It goes against the natural laws that we take for granted. It is certainly wonderful to see. Consequently, throughout history people have gained comfort from the fact that miracles can be understood and explained in terms of the religious or cultural traditions of the times and the areas where they occurred.

I believe that there are two sorts of miracles:

1. Miracles that can be credited to divine intervention, and

2. Miracles that we create ourselves.

A friend related an example of the first type of miracle to me a few months ago. His mother was seriously ill in the hospital, and was not expected to survive. My friend went into a church for the first time in more than twenty years and prayed to God. His mother recovered completely and lived for another twelve years. My friend is totally convinced that God answered his prayer and healed his mother.

The fact that we are alive could be considered a miracle, but the fact that we have the power to change and mold our lives to become whatever we want to be is even more of a miracle. It is this second type of miracle that we will be mainly concerned with in this book. Incidentally, according to Webster's dictionary, Christian Science can claim credit for this view of the miraculous. Members of this sect believe that we all have the power to become miracle workers, once we cease believing that this concept is impossible.

We will start with a look at religious miracles, as this is what most people think about when the subject is raised. The second chapter covers healing miracles. This is the type of miracle most people seek when they request a miracle. Chapter 3 focuses on how you can attract miracles into your own life. The remainder of the book covers a variety of methods and techniques you can use to transform your life, and make every day a miraculous one. Resolve that you will experience miracles on a regular basis, practice the different techniques in this book, and make it happen.

One

Religious Miracles

BECAUSE MIRACLES ARE usually attributed to some form of divine intervention, it is not surprising that miracles figure prominently in the histories of all the great religions. In fact, according to the Apostle Paul, if it had not been for the miracle of Christ's Resurrection, Christianity would not be worth considering. In the first letter to the Corinthians he wrote: "And if Christ be not risen, then is our preaching vain, and your faith is also vain." (1 Corinthians 15:14). Willa Sibert Cather wrote, "The Miracles of the Church seem to me to rest not so much upon faces or voices or healing power coming suddenly near to us from afar off, but upon our perceptions being made finer, so that for a moment our eyes can see and our ears can hear what is there about us always."[1]

A typical example of a religious miracle is when God halted the sun in the sky for an entire day to give Joshua, Moses' successor, more time to defeat the Amorites (Joshua 10: 12–14). If night had fallen when it should have, the Amorites would have been able to escape. Of course, if this miracle actually occurred, God must have temporarily suspended other natural laws as well. Otherwise, everything would have been tossed off the earth when it stopped turning for several hours to allow the miracle to occur. From a scientific standpoint, the earth could not stop turning for a whole day, but, with a miracle, anything is possible.

Obviously, a miracle of this sort can not be proved or disproved thousands of years later. There is no way of knowing if it happened exactly as recorded in the Bible, or if a smaller event was exaggerated for effect. It is even possible that the story was fictitious, and was written solely to give people a sense of the miraculous. One remarkable aspect of this miracle, is that Joshua asked God to stop the movement of the sun, and God acted on his request.

Biblically, there are three purposes to a religious miracle:

1. To glorify God (John 2:11; 11:40),

2. To appoint certain people to speak for God (Hebrews 2:4), and

3. To provide evidence for belief in God (John 6:2; 6:14; 20:30–31).

In the Bible, there are five main aspects to a miracle:

1. Miracles are unusual. They create awe and wonder. A burning bush, and the ability to walk on water, are not everyday occurrences.

2. Miracles are an act of God. This presupposes that there is a God who created the universe.

3. Miracles reflect God. Because God is good, miracles promote goodness.

4. Miracles frequently confirm the truth of God through a servant of God (Hebrews 2:4). Consequently, they reveal genuine prophets.

5. Miracles are always done with a purpose in mind. They glorify God, and at the same time prove the existence of God.

Obviously, the greatest miracle of all for Christians is the Incarnation, when God became Man. It is a central doctrine of the Christian church that God became man in Jesus Christ. This means that Jesus was both God and man, and was a combination of both divine and human natures. As John the Evangelist said: "the Word was made flesh" (John 1:14). The Council of Nicaea (325 CE) concluded that Christ was "begotten, not made," which meant he was Creator, rather than creature. The Council of Chalcedon (451 CE)came to the conclusion that Jesus was perfect in both deity and humanity.[2] Neither nature was diluted by this union, and the essential identity of each was fully preserved. C. S. Lewis called this "the Grand Miracle."[3]

Obviously, people who believe that Jesus Christ is the son of God also believe in miracles, as this instance of God becoming flesh and living in the world is by any standards a "Grand Miracle." However, Soren Kierkegaard (1813–1855), the Danish theologian, wrote that "the miracle can prove nothing; for if you do not believe that he is what he says he is, you deny the miracle."[4]

Biblical Miracles

The Bible is considered a sacred book by Christians, Jews, and Muslims. The word Bible comes from the Greek word *biblia*, which means "books." These collections of "books" vary from faith to faith, and even within faiths. The Catholic Bible includes the Apocrypha, for instance. The Apocrypha is not considered a canonical text by the protestant and orthodox Christian religions.

The Jewish version of the Bible is called the Tanakh. It consists of thirty-nine books from the Old Testament, which are arranged in a different order to that of the Christian Bible. Also, of course, the Tanakh is interpreted with the aid of an oral Torah that was given to Moses, and passed on by rote. It was finally written down in the early centuries of the Christian Era and is known as the Mishnah and the Talmud.

The Muslims, like the Jews and Christians, consider themselves to be spiritual descendants of Abraham. Their main text, of course, is The Koran. However, they consider three sections of the Bible to be divine revelation: the first five books (Pentateuch), the psalms, and the gospels.

Interestingly, there is no word in the Hebrew Bible that relates to the word "miracle."[5] This is because God's intervention could explain anything that happened. Of course, the Hebrews were well aware of the many instances that inspired awe or wonder, and the Bible is full of accounts of these.

When the angel of the Lord appeared to Moses in the form of a burning bush, that was not consumed by the flames, Moses had a sense of both awe and wonder. However, he did not describe it as a miracle. This was but the first of a series of miraculous events that occurred involving Moses and the chosen people. The most dramatic of these was when the waters of the Red Sea parted to allow the Israelites to escape Pharaoh's army, who were swallowed up in the sea (Exodus 14: 21–29). This miracle finally freed the Israelites, proving once and for all, that they were in fact God's chosen people.

This is obviously a huge miracle, but the Bible also contains many instances of small miracles that show God's compassion for everyday people. Elisha presided over a small community of prophets. One of these died, and his widow was threatened by a creditor who said he would take her two children and sell them into slavery to satisfy the debt. The widow came to Elisha for help. He asked her what she had in the house. All she had, she told him, was a pot of oil. Elisha told her to borrow as many vessels as she could from her friends and neighbors and to pour oil from her pot into them. To the widow's amazement, the oil in her pot filled all the other containers, and her pot remained full. When she told Elisha what had happened, he told her to sell the oil. This gave her enough money to pay off her debts, with plenty left over to live on (2 Kings 4:1–7).

This story is similar to the story of Jesus and the loaves and fishes. With five loaves of bread and two fish, Jesus was able to feed five thousand people (Matthew 14:15–21; Mark 6:38–44; Luke 9:13–17; John 6:1–14).

Jesus, of course, performed many miracles, starting with the turning of water into wine at the wedding in Cana, Galilee (John 2:1–11). This miracle is unlike his later miracles, and was probably performed reluctantly, as he told his mother that his hour was not yet come. He performed many healings, including healing someone who was deaf and dumb. He cured the lame and blind. He cured lepers. He restored a number of people to life. The most famous example of this is when he raised Lazarus from the dead at Bethany (John 11:38–44). Another example is when he restored a widow's only son to life at Nain (Luke 7:11–17). He also brought the twelve-year-old daughter of Jairus back to life (Matthew 9:24–25; Mark 5:35–43; Luke 8:41–56).

One of the most delightful of the miracles of Jesus was when he walked on water. At first, the disciples were afraid, as they thought it was a spirit walking across the sea toward them. Once they were reassured, Peter immediately asked if he could walk on the water, too. Jesus said, "Come," and Peter stepped out of the boat. When he saw the waves he became afraid and began to sink. "Immediately Jesus stretched forth his hand, and caught him, and said unto him, O thou of little faith, wherefore didst thou doubt?" (Matthew 14: 25–31)

Most of Jesus' miracles were acts of compassion. Two thousand years ago, illness was believed to be a divine punishment for some wrongdoing. Jesus' healings not only restored the sufferers' health, but also removed the huge load of guilt they were carrying.

Not surprisingly, being the son of God, Jesus was able to perform miracles at will, any time he wished. The only time he appeared to have any difficulty was when he returned to his home town and experienced the disbelief of the inhabitants. Jesus mildly said, "A prophet is not without honor, but in his own country, and among his own kin, and in his own house." (Mark 6:4)

Despite the skepticism and disbelief, "he laid his hands upon a few sick folk, and healed them." (Mark 6:5)

Of course, the Resurrection of Jesus is the ultimate Christian miracle. It represented triumph over death, and promised eternal life to everyone who believed in him. The Roman and Jewish authorities would have produced the body if they had taken it away for some reason. The apostles suffered enormous hardship and persecution when they told people about the resurrection of Christ. They would not have persevered with their claims if they had removed Jesus' body.

There were more than five hundred witnesses to Jesus' resurrection. Jesus appeared first to Mary Magdalene (John 20:14–18). He then appeared to Mary Magdalene again, this time with the other Mary as a witness (Matthew 28:9–10). He appeared to Simon Peter (Luke 24:34), to two disciples on their way to Emmaus (Luke 24:13–32), and to ten apostles (John 20:19–25). Thomas was not present on that occasion, and said that unless he could see the print of the nails in his hands, and touch them, he would not believe (John 20:24–25). Eight days later, Jesus appeared to the eleven apostles, including Thomas (John 20:26–29). He then appeared to Simon Peter, Thomas, Nathaniel, the two sons of Zebedee, and two other disciples at the Sea of Tiberias (John 21:1–14). He also appeared again to the eleven apostles to prepare them for their future role (Matthew 28:16–20), to "above five hundred brethren at once" (1 Corinthians 15:6), to his brother James (1 Corinthians 15:7), and to his disciples at the ascension (Luke 24:50–53; Acts 1:4–11).

Despite these miracles, not everyone believed. John wrote: "But though he had done so many miracles before them, yet they believed not on him" (John 12:37). Jesus Himself said: "Neither will they be persuaded, though one rose from the dead" (Luke 16:31).

Some people have expressed doubt about the miracles of Jesus, while others feel he is purely a mythical figure. Of course, if the gospel stories are purely fiction, it would be reasonable to wonder why Jesus was portrayed in the way he was. Surely, he'd be shown as an all-powerful wizard who would produce much more astounding miracles than the ones he is credited with. For instance, when he walked on water, he did it at night, and only his disciples witnessed it. If he had been looking for maximum impact, he would have done this in daylight when a large number of people would have seen it.

The apostles of Jesus were also able to perform miracles in His name. Peter and John healed a lame man who asked them for alms as they entered the gate of a temple. Peter said to him: "Silver and gold have I none; but such as I have give I thee: In the name of Jesus Christ of Nazareth rise up and walk." Peter took hold of the man's right hand and helped him to his feet. Immediately, this man who had been lame from birth began "walking, and leaping, and praising God." (Acts 3: 2–8).

The story of Simon the sorcerer is an interesting one, as he offered the apostles gold to teach him how to perform miracles. The Bible says: "And when Simon saw that through laying on of the apostles' hands the Holy Ghost was given, he offered them money, saying, 'Give me also this power, that on whomsoever I lay hands, he may receive the Holy Ghost.' But Peter said unto him, 'Thy money perish with thee, because thou hast thought that the gift of God may be purchased with money. Thou hast neither part nor lot in this matter: for thy heart is not right in the sight of God.'" (Acts 8: 18–21) This shows that the ability to perform miracles is dependent on faith, rather than money.

Saint Paul was responsible for many miraculous healings, including bringing a young man called Eutychus back to life. Eutychus was sitting in a window on the third story of a house, listening to Saint Paul preach. Unfortunately, he fell asleep during the long sermon and fell out the window. Everyone rushed to his aid, but it was too late. The fall had killed him. Saint Paul "fell on him, and embracing him said, Trouble not yourselves; for his life is in him." Eutychus immediately sat up, had something to eat and drink, and talked until the morning (Acts 20: 9–12).

Miracles of the Saints

Although Jesus and his disciples never mentioned the word "saint," people who appear to have a special relationship with God, along with moral perfection, and a quality of holiness, appear in all of the major religions, and are termed "saints." These people are frequently seers, prophets, teachers, priests, priestesses, or religious teachers.

Saints were recognized as early as one hundred years after the death of Christ, when people began venerating the martyrs as saints. People believed that these martyrs went straight to heaven and could therefore be effective intercessors for the living.

In the tenth century, Pope John XV initiated a procedure of canonization. This gradually developed into a set process in which any candidates to sainthood had to have led an exemplary, holy life, and have performed at least two miracles. Consequently, entire libraries could be filled with books relating the miracles of the saints.

An interesting example of this is the apparent immunity to fire possessed by Saint Francis of Paola (1416–1507), the founder of the Minim friars. On one occasion, Francis visited a blacksmith to have some work done. The blacksmith was busy, and Francis asked if their would be enough iron left over for his job. The smith indicated a large piece of red-hot iron that was available. Francis picked it up, and when the smith screamed at him to drop it, replied that he was holding it to keep himself warm.

On another occasion, he helped some men make charcoal. Unfortunately, the workmen did not do a good job, and flames were coming through the earth that they had placed over the wood. While the men found more earth, Francis controlled the flames with his bare feet.

Francis was also able to transfer his immunity to other people. The furnace of a lime kiln seemed about to collapse. As the entrance was too small for Francis to enter, he asked a smaller monk to crawl in and prop up the ceiling with a stick. The monk was able to do this task, without receiving any injuries.[6]

Saint Don Bosco (1815–1888) was canonized in 1934. In 1860, he and his mother were running a hostel for homeless youths in Turin, Italy. One morning, while hearing confessions, he was told that there were not enough breakfast rolls to feed the more than three hundred children in his care. Don Bosco quietly told the house matrons to collect all the food that was available, and he would distribute it personally. Francisco Dalmazzo, a boy who was staying in the house, later testified that Don Bosco started with a basket of fifteen to twenty rolls, which never seemed to reduce in quantity, as Don Bosco handed every child a roll.[7] This miracle was in essence a duplication of the one Jesus performed when he fed five thousand people with five loaves of bread and two fish (Matthew 14:14–21; Mark 6: 35–44; John 6: 5–14).

Throughout his life, Don Bosco was protected by a phantom dog called Gerigio who would attack anyone who tried to harm the priest. On one occasion Gerigio turned on the priest when he tried to leave the hostel. Shortly afterward, a friend arrived to warn Don Bosco of a threat on his life. Many people tried to explain the mystery of Gerigio. One of the more likely explanations is that Don Bosco's angel guardian assumed the appearance of a large dog whenever necessary, as this was the form most likely to be of help.[8]

Jean-Baptiste-Marie Vianney (1786–1859) also fed a multitude with very little food. One day he discovered that he had virtually no wheat to make bread for the orphanage he had established in Ars, France. He placed a small relic of a saint into the wheat and prayed. The following morning the granary was so full of wheat that people thought the ancient wooden floor would give way under the weight of it. On another occasion, there was only enough flour to make three loaves of bread, rather than the ten that were required. Jean told the cook to pray and bake the bread. To her astonishment, she produced ten huge loaves of bread, each weighing between twenty and twenty-two pounds. When she told Jean what she had managed to produce, he reportedly replied: "God is very good. He looks after the poor!"[9]

Saint Jean Vianney made an interesting prediction about himself in 1852. His achievements made it a foregone conclusion he would become a saint, but he said that the canonization ceremony would be delayed by war. He was beatified in 1905, and would have been canonized in 1914. However, the First World War meant that he did not achieve this goal until 1925 when he was canonized as the patron saint of parish priests.

Saint Bruno (c. 1030–1101), founder of the Carthusian Order, did not multiply food, but had the ability to transform poultry into tortoises. One Friday, Saint Bruno arrived at a monastery and found all the monks sitting before plates of fowl. No one knew what to do, as they were forbidden to eat fowl on Fridays. Saint Bruno sat down at the table, made the sign of the cross over the forbidden food and transformed them all into tortoises, a meal that the monks were allowed to eat.[10]

Probably the most incredible miracle of food conversion involved Saint Nicholas of Tolentino (1245–1305). As Nicholas lay dying, his colleagues couldn't help but notice how thin he had become. They decided to entice him into eating by preparing a special meal of dressed doves. However, Nicholas was a vegetarian, and would not eat the meal. He sat up in bed and waved his hands over the dish. Instantly, the doves were restored to life and flew out the window, where they hovered until Saint Nicholas finally died a few days later. The monks believed that the doves transported his soul to Heaven.[11]

Bilocation

Throughout history, a small number of holy people have been able to be in two places at the same time. This phenomenon is called bilocation. One of the most famous examples of this is Saint Alfonso de Liguori (1696–1787). On September 22, 1774, Alfonso was meditating while locked in a prison cell in Arezzo, Italy. After his meditation, he told the fellow prisoners that Pope Clement XIV had just died. The inmates were skeptical, because Alfonso had obviously not left his cell, and Rome was more than a day's journey away. However, a day or two later, word came that the pope had died, and Alfonso had been seen participating in prayer vigils at the bedside of the dying man.

Another well-known example is Saint Anthony of Padua (1195–1231). Saint Anthony was preaching at a church in Limoges on Holy Thursday in 1226 when he suddenly remembered that he was supposed to be conducting a service at a monastery on the other side of the city. He knelt down and prayed, watched by his congregation. At the same instant, the monks at the monastery saw Saint Anthony step forward to conduct the service. When he had finished, he returned to his stall in the chapel. Immediately after this, the congregation at the first church saw him get up from his prayers and finish the service.

One of the strange aspects of bilocation is that the person can eat, drink, and do anything else he or she wishes, but in two different places simultaneously. One of these people is not an apparition. Neither is it an instance of an out-of-body experience, in which the astral body is seen by others. The person temporarily exists in two bodies at the same time.

Saint Martin de Porres (1579–1639) demonstrated that distance has no bearing on bilocation, as he was seen in two different countries simultaneously. He spent his entire life in Peru, but was seen in both Japan and China. Saint Martin frequently expressed his desire to work as a missionary in the Far East. Saint Martin also visited a Spanish man in his prison cell in Algiers and gave him enough money to pay his ransom. This man, who had been imprisoned by the Turks, was overwhelmed when he visited Lima and saw Saint Martin at the monastery of the Holy Rosary.[12]

Mary of Agreda, a seventeenth-century nun, was told by her superiors to stop talking about her visits to Indian tribes in New Mexico, because everyone knew that she had never left her native country, Spain. However, at the same time, Father Alonzo de Benavides in New Mexico, wrote a letter to the Pope to tell him about the "lady in blue" who had given the Indians a variety of items, including a chalice, to use when celebrating Mass. Amazingly, the chalice had come from Mary's convent in Spain.[13]

Followers of Satya Sai Baba attest to the fact that he is able to bilocate himself. Two researchers from the American Society for Psychical Research, Karlis Osis and Erlendur Haraldsson, visited India on a number of occasions to investigate these claims. They were skeptical about some of the claims of Sai Baba, but were impressed with the bilocation skills of another mystic, Dadaji. In 1970, Dadaji was visiting some devotees in Allahabad. At the same time, he bilocated to a home in Calcutta. Roma Mukherjee, the daughter of the household, was reading a book when Dadaji appeared. Initially, Dadaji was almost transparent, but the apparition quickly became more solid, and Dadaji asked her to bring him a cup of tea. Dadaji drank this, and smoked half a cigarette, before disappearing.[14]

Bilocation is a rare phenomenon, but one that can certainly be classed as a miracle. Saint Martin de Porres was quite matter of fact about his skills in this direction. When someone asked him about it, he is believed to have replied that if God could multiply the fishes and loaves of bread, He could certainly duplicate him.

Levitation

The Roman Catholic Church records show that more than two hundred saints have overcome the laws of gravity and levitated. In fact, there are so many recorded instances of levitation, that the Catholic Church no longer considers this strange ability to be evidence of saintliness. In fact, at times, the involuntary levitation of priests and monks has proved an embarrassment. Joseph of Copertino (1603–1663) is a good example. Joseph's levitations became so famous that he became known as the "flying friar." He had always been considered difficult, and while staying at a monastery before facing charges of heresy, several nuns saw Joseph soar through the air from a corner of the chapel to the altar, and back again. The next recorded instance of his levitation skills was when he knelt on the ground to kiss the feet of Pope Urban III. Instead of kissing the pontiff's feet he went into a state of rapture and rose several feet into the air. While in Assisi, he soared fifteen feet over the heads of other worshippers to kiss a painting of the Virgin Mary.

The most famous levitation story about Joseph occurred when he was strolling round a monastery garden with the Reverend Antonio Chiarello. When Chiarello remarked on the beauty of the heaven that God had made, Joseph cried out in ecstasy and immediately soared into the air, alighting on the very top of an olive tree. The people who witnessed this levitation commented with amazement that the branch he landed on shook only slightly, as if a small bird had alighted on it, rather than a fully grown man. Joseph remained in a state of rapture for a whole hour, before returning to his normal self. The other monks needed a stepladder to get him down.

On one occasion, Joseph levitated a bystander with him. During a special service in the Church of Santa Chiara in Copertino, Joseph was on his knees praying, when the priest conducting the service said, "Come, Bride of Christ." Joseph immediately ran toward a priest from Secli, who happened to be at the service, grasped his hand and levitated into the air, taking the startled priest with him.[15]

Fortunately, although he experienced persecution at first, the church came to accept Joseph's levitations as the work of God. Even when he was dying, the doctor who attended him noticed that Joseph was floating six inches above his bed.[16]

Saint Teresa of Avila (1515–1582) was famous for her levitations. However, these involuntary levitations caused her extreme embarrassment. Whenever she felt she was about to levitate she would ask her fellow sisters to hold her down.

Levitation is not purely the prerogative of saints. The Frank-furter Zeitung of September 8, 1861 contained an article about a service at the Church of St. Mary, in Vienna, the previous Sunday. "Soon after the commencement of the sermon, a girl of about twenty years of age, showed all signs of ecstasy, and soon, her arms crossed across her bosom, and with her eyes fixed on the preacher, she was seen by the whole congregation to be raised gradually from the floor into the air, and there to rest at an eleva-tion of more than a foot until the end of the sermon. We are assured that the same phenomenon had happened several days previously at the moment of her receiving the communion."

Levitation is rarer outside of religious circles. However, the English medium, Daniel Dunglas Home, was reputed to have lev-itated on at least one hundred occasions, sometimes while stand-ing, and at other times while sitting in a chair. In the latter instances, the chair usually levitated with him.

Relics

Relics have played an important role in many religions. Examples include fragments of the cross of Jesus, the sacred tooth of Bud-dha, and the hairs of the prophet Muhammad.

Sacred relics began early in the Christian Church. In 326 CE, Helena, mother of Emperor Constantine, went on a pilgrimage to Palestine. While there, a pious Jew took her to the place that was believed to be where Jesus had been crucified. When the ground was dug up, three crosses were found. Helena wanted to find out which cross had held Jesus. According to one version of this story, a dead body was placed upon each cross in turn. It miraculously came back to life when placed on the cross of Jesus. Other versions say that a sick woman was restored to health when she touched the cross of Jesus. Helena took half of the cross, along with the crown of thorns, and the nails that had been used to fasten Jesus to the cross, back to Rome, making them the first religious relics of the Christian church.[17]

Relics were originally objects for pious devotion, but it did not take long for miracles to be reported that were credited to them. St. Augustine reported that some seventy miracles were recorded at the relics of St. Stephen at Hippo-Regius, alone. In his Confessions, St. Augustine mentioned many miracles that were performed by relics. For instance, a blind man in Milan had his sight restored when he touched the cloth that covered the bones of two early martyrs, Protavius and Gervasius.

Hundreds of thousands of similar cures credited to relics were reported in the Middle Ages.[18] The churches that housed these religious relics made huge sums of money from them, and this encouraged other churches to fraudulently claim that they had genuine relics, too. As people became more educated, belief in relics declined.

Shrines

Sacred shrines are still popular places of pilgrimage. In medieval times, large numbers of sick and infirm people made lengthy pilgrimages to the shrines of the saints at Glastonbury, Lindisfarne, Canterbury, Westminster, St. Albans, and many other places, seeking a miraculous cure. Sometimes, a miracle occurred. Over five hundred miracles occurred at the shrine of St. Thomas à Becket. Thirty-nine people were alleged to have been raised from the dead at the Church of the Holy Rood of Bronholm in Norfolk, and a further twelve were cured of blindness.[19]

The Stigmata

The stigmata is the occurrence of wounds that replicate those of Christ on the cross. Blood appears in the hands and feet, and sometimes also on the right-hand side where Jesus was pierced by a lance, and the forehead where he wore a crown of thorns. Amazingly, the wounds appear and vanish again, usually opening again on specific occasions, such as Good Friday or Christmas day. Although in some cases the wounds remain open for long periods of time, infection never occurs.

The first person known to receive a stigmata was St. Francis of Assisi, who gained the wounds in 1224, while praying on top of Mount Alvernus. He tried to conceal them from his followers, but it was impossible. However, although Saint Francis is generally credited with being the first, it is possible that Saint Paul was a stigmatic. In his Epistle to the Galatians (6:17) he wrote: "From henceforth let no man trouble me: for I bear in my body the marks of the Lord Jesus."

Since then, there have been many accounts of stigmatics. The wounds seem to appear as a result of religious ecstasy. A Bavarian woman, Teresa Neumann (1898–1962) received the stigmata every Friday for thirty-two years, starting at Easter 1926. Amazingly, she lost up to a pint of blood every time the stigmata occurred. While in a trance state, she would lie completely rigid in bed, and relive every moment of Calvary and the crucifixion. Apparently, she was also able to speak Aramaic, and other languages, while in this state, even though she could not speak them normally. She was able to answer questions while in a trance, and apparently her descriptions of Jerusalem at the time of Jesus was an accurate one. The stigmata would last for a day or two, but Teresa would be fully restored, and able to go to church, on Sundays. She wore white gloves to conceal her scars.[20]

Another well known stigmatic was Padre Pio da Pietrelcina (1887–1968). One day, on September 20, 1918, Padre Pio was alone in the chapel of a monastery in San Giovanni Rotondo. Mass was over, but Padre Pio was still on his knees in front of a statue of the crucifixion. Suddenly, the other friars heard him screaming with pain. When they found him, blood was coming from deep holes in his hands and feet, and from a wound in his left chest. These wounds never healed. They would become covered with scabs for a while, but then start bleeding again.

The Catholic church was not happy with the attention the stigmata gave to the young priest. Newspaper reports of the time mention the long lines of people who wanted to confess only to Padre Pio.[21] On July 5, 1923, the Sacred Congregation of the Holy Office declared that what had happened to Padre Pio had not been proved to be supernatural in origin. This did not resolve the situation. Books about Padre Pio were banned, and an attempt to remove him from San Giovanni Rotondo failed when the local inhabitants threatened to use force, if necessary.

A cult grew around Padre Pio, especially when he seemed able to heal at a distance. He was also able to bilocate, appearing to people all over Europe, while at the same time being seen at San Giovanni Rotondo. People usually smelled a strong perfume when he made these appearances.

One of his healings concerned a farmer from Padua who had embolisms on both lungs. He prayed for help, and an apparition of a bearded monk appeared. He placed his hand on the farmer's chest, smiled, and then disappeared. The farmer immediately felt that he had been cured, and this proved to be the case. A few months later he saw a photograph of the monk who had appeared to him, and discovered that it was Padre Pio. He immediately went to Foggia, attended morning Mass and then went to Confession with Padre Pio. Before he had an opportunity to introduce himself, and explain why he was there, Padre Pio asked: "And tell me, what about the lungs now? How are they?"[22]

An even more remarkable miracle occurred when, in 1929, Padre Pio healed Dr. Ricciardi, a man who considered Padre Pio to be a fraud. When Dr. Ricciardi contracted an incurable brain tumor, he told his relatives that he wanted to die in peace, and especially did not want to see any priests. If any came to visit, he wanted them thrown out of the house. One day, when the doctor was close to death, he opened his eyes to see Padre Pio at the entrance of his bedroom. Padre Pio entered the room and began praying in Latin, asking for peace for the house and everyone who lived in it. When he had finished, he asked the doctor if he would accept from him the holy oil that he used to anoint the dying. The doctor agreed.

"Your soul is right," Padre Pio said. "And in just a few days your body too will be right again."

Padre Pio proved correct, and Dr. Ricciardi was restored to perfect health.[23] Padre Pio was also famous for his skills at bilocation, and in 1942 bilocated to the bedside of a dying friend, Monsignor Damiani, in Salto, Uruguay.

Many stigmatics also produce red rings that encircle the flesh of the ring finger. These are called espousal rings, and the people who receive them believe that they were placed on their fingers by Christ. Marie-Julie Jahenny is an example of a stigmatic who received an espousal ring in 1873, when she was twenty-three. The ring never disappeared, and ultimately looked as if it was made of red coral.[24]

There have been more than three hundred reported cases of stigmatization. Most of these people have been women.[25] Naturally, most of these cases have occurred in deeply religious people, but a small number of nonreligious stigmatizations have been recorded.

In the Islamic religion, stigmatizations have also occurred. These stigmatas appeared on people who had been contemplating the battle wounds of the prophet Muhammad.[26]

Not surprisingly, the phenomenon of stigmata has been thoroughly investigated over the years. Not everyone credits it to divine intervention. One argument for this is that the exact location of the stigmata varies from person to person, and frequently corresponds to those shown on an image of Christ that is familiar to the stigmatic. Some people say that the stigmata is caused in people who find it hard to live up to the imagined ideals of a Christian life. Others feel that it is a punishment for unreconciled sexual urges. No matter what the cause of the stigmata is, the actual wounds behave in a highly mysterious manner. They can not be healed by contemporary medical science, neither do they become inflamed or infected. Some stigmatics bleed constantly, while others bleed only on significant days, such as Fridays and Sundays.

Bleeding Statues

How is it possible for plaster statues of the Madonna to cry? Or similar statues of Christ bleed? In 1968, a life-size wooden statue of Christ in Porto das Caixas in Brazil started bleeding, to the consternation of the altar boy who discovered it. This crucifix was three-hundred years old. The day after it was discovered, the first healing miracle was reported. By 1976, eight of many miracles that had been performed by the statue were ratified by a commission set up by Archbishop Antonio de Almeida Moraes. The blood was tested by Dr Enias Heringer and found to be genuine.[27]

In 1974, a statue of the Virgin at Caltanisetta, Sicily, started bleeding from the right cheek. It stopped for some years, and started again in 1981.

In 1975, Dr. Joseph Rovito x-rayed a plaster statue that bled from the hands on Fridays and other holy days. The bleeding would continue unabated for up to four hours. Dr. Rovito was astounded at what he discovered. The blood was genuine, but had an extremely low red blood cell count, indicating that it was extremely old.[28]

There have been many other instances of weeping and bleeding statues. There has also been at least one instance of a bleeding postcard of Jesus. The fascinating aspect of all of these is that the tears and blood flow from the sites that one would expect. Tears come from the Virgin's eyes, while blood appears from the forehead, hands, feet, and side of Jesus.

It has been argued that these strange manifestations are caused unconsciously by the strong faith of their owners. However, even if this proves to be the case, this phenomenon is still miraculous.

Islamic Miracles

The miracles attributed to Jesus are central to the Christian faith. The miracles attributed to Muhammad are not an integral part of the Islamic faith, and appear to be purely incidental to his life and teachings. In fact, in some books Muhammad's miracles appear in the form of lists, instead of being described in detail. A notable example of this is the listing of forty-five miracles in Book XX of the *Ihya' 'ulum ad-din* by the medieval theologian, Abu Hamid al-Ghazzali, who died in 1111 CE.[29]

The first miracle listed is a famous one in which Muhammad divided the Moon into two halves, so that Mount Hira could be seen between them. He did this to convince his enemies, the Quraysh, that his revelations were true.

On a number of occasions the Prophet fed large groups of people with small amounts of food. For instance, he fed more than eighty men with four barley cakes that could be held in one hand. On another occasion, Muhammad noticed that the provisions of the army he was with had become extremely low. He asked for everything to be brought to him. He blessed it, and then had it redistributed. Every vessel in the camp became completely full.

He produced water from wells that were dry. On another occasion, water appeared from between his fingers, and he was able to quench the thirst of an entire army. The ability to produce water in desert regions cannot be overemphasized.

He blinded an enemy army by blowing a handful of dust at them. He summoned two trees, who came to him and joined together, until he ordered them to separate.

Muhammad performed healing miracles, as well. An eye of one of his companions became dislodged, and was hanging on his cheek. Muhammad put it back into its socket, and it was fully restored. Muhammad restored the injured foot of one of his companions by rubbing it.

On one occasion he did the opposite. He asked a father if he could take his daughter in marriage. Rather than saying "no," the father told him that she had leprosy. Muhammad said, "Let it be so," and the woman immediately became leprous.

Muhammad's Night Journey and Ascension are the most important aspects of his life. The Night Journey tells how the Archangel Gabriel summoned Muhammad and took him on a winged horse to Jerusalem, where he met all the earlier prophets, from Adam to Jesus. Muhammad led them all in prayer, demonstrating his precedence over all the others.

After this, he paid a visit to heaven. There are many accounts of Muhammad's Ascension. In all versions, Gabriel takes Muhammad through the various levels of heaven, meeting different prophets along the way. He spoke with Adam in the first heaven, and John the Baptist and Jesus in the second. He talked with Moses and Abraham in the sixth heaven. He then climbed the Tree of Life and saw four rivers, two visible and two hidden. Gabriel told him that the two hidden rivers are in Paradise, and the two visible rivers are the Nile and the Euphrates. Muhammad was then brought containers of wine, milk, and honey, demonstrating that the land of the Arabs was holy, and contained milk and honey, exactly the same as that promised to the ancient Hebrews. The climax of the Ascension is when Muhammad saw God. Some accounts say that Muhammad saw God directly, while others say that he saw God through a cloud.

In some versions of the Ascension, Muhammad asked to see a glimpse of hell, and was shown the torment of the people condemned to spend eternity there.

The Night Journey and the Ascension play a special role in Islam. They demonstrate that Muhammad is the greatest of all the prophets, someone privileged enough to see both heaven and hell. Most importantly, of course, Muhammad also saw God.

Muhammad was also granted a special favor at the end of his life. When Azrael, the angel of death, came to him, Muhammad asked for an extra hour as he wanted to speak to Gabriel. Gabriel arrived with 70,000 angels in attendance, and they sang verses from the Holy Book. Archangel Michael also visited, bearing verses from the Holy Book. Muhammad said goodbye to Fatima, his wife, and told her that she would be joining him in six months. He said goodbye to his children and grandchildren. He then closed his eyes and died.

The Muslim religion accepts miracles, and believes that Allah worked miracles through Moses, Solomon, and Jesus. Interestingly, the prophet Muhammad did not claim to perform miracles. He considered the Koran to be the greatest miracle, and he was simply a human messenger.[30] Despite this, his birth and life have been shrouded with a number of miraculous details.

Miracles are mentioned rarely in the Koran. The word for miracle in the Koran is Çya, which means an apparent sign or mark by which something is known. In Sutra 6:109, we read: "They swear their strongest oaths by Allah that if a sign came to them, by it they would believe. Say: 'Certainly, Signs are in the power of Allah but what will make you realize that if Signs came, they will not believe.'"[31] "Signs are in the power of Allah" shows that extraordinary signs would occur to provide evidence of the Prophet's divine mission.

Islamic mystics, known as *Sufis*, believe implicitly in miracles, and make pilgrimages to the tombs of saints who have the power to provide *barakah* (blessings), even after death. The cult of saints plays an important role in popular belief. A number of tombs of saints have been destroyed by religious zealots who believe that the cult of saints is not part of true Islam.

Jewish Miracles

There is an old Jewish proverb that says: "He who does not believe in miracles is not a realist." Many miracles are recorded in the Talmud, a collection of Jewish law, legend, and lore, as well as in the scriptures.

In Jewish tradition it is believed that miracles can be obtained by using the nine names of God that are found in the Sephiroth, the ten states of being in the Kabbalah. This comes from the opening sentence of the Gospel According to John, which reads: "In the beginning was the Word, and the Word was with God, and the Word was God." (John 1:1) However, the names in the Sephiroth are actually substitutes for the secret names, so it must have been the belief of the people who recited these names that caused miracles to occur. The nine names are:

Ehieh (or Emet)
Iod
Tetragrammaton Elohi
El
Elohim Gebor
Eloah Va-Daath
El Adonai Tzabaoth
Elohim Tzabaoth
Shaddai (or El Chai)

El is Hebrew for God, and Elohim is the plural form. Interestingly, when Moses asked God for His name, the reply was: "I am that I am." (Exodus 3:14)

The Kabbalists were interested in miracles. Rabbinic Judaism was not greatly interested in miracles, as it was mainly interested in doing God's will according to his Law. However, the Hasidic movement, which began in the eighteenth century, had a strong belief in the magical power and miracles of the Hasidic saints and rabbis.[32]

Buddhist Miracles

Gautama Buddha performed a number of miracles, but tended to play them down as he felt they lacked spiritual significance. Despite this, the cosmos spontaneously caused miraculous phenomena to occur at important moments in his life, including birth, enlightenment, and death. These included earthquakes, flowers pouring down from heaven, the sprouting of jewel-laden trees, and the appearance of beautifully perfumed rivers.

The saints in Buddhism were also surrounded by miraculous phenomena, and appeared to be almost supernatural. They could control time and space, life and death, and appeared to have total control over the entire cosmos. Mahakasyapa, a disciple of Buddha, is a good example of a Buddhist saint. He was able to fly magically, perform transformations, and teach both humans and supernatural beings.[33]

After Buddha's death, relics associated with him were credited with performing countless miracles. According to the Anguttara Nikaya, a collection of Buddha's sayings, he taught that there were three kinds of miracles: the miracle of magic, the miracle of mind reading, and the miracle of instruction. Buddha considered the miracle of instruction to be the most important of these, and felt the first two were not much more than conjuror's tricks.

In Tibet, magical, and often talking, images of the goddess Tara are said to possess miraculous power. Tara is believed to guard and protect Tibetans from birth until after death. Not surprisingly, she is hugely popular, and people share both their joys and sorrows with her. There are many stories of the incredible powers that images of her can provide.

One good example concerns a destitute man who found an image of Tara on a rock. He immediately knelt down and prayed to her. When he got up, the image pointed to a shrine. He dug a hole where she indicated, and found a jar full of jewels. The destitute man was now extremely wealthy, but he used the money to help others, and for seven generations poverty disappeared. As his reward, he enjoyed many incarnations in which he lived to become a wealthy old man.[34]

Another example concerns a servant who was attacked by a wild yak. Normally, the man would have been gored by the horns, but because he was carrying an image of Tara, the yak's horns bent against his body and did no harm.

In 1968, an article in the Tibetan news magazine *Shes-bya* reported that an Englishman had bought an image of Tara, and had attempted to illegally take it out of Nepal. However, when he tried to board his plane, the bag containing the image became heavier and heavier, until he could no longer lift it. This alerted customs officials who confiscated the image.[35]

Religious miracles are important, as they reveal the power and potential of the particular religion to the population at large. However, for most people, a personal miracle, such as the healing of an illness, was much more important. We will look at healing miracles in the next chapter.

Two

Healing Miracles

Miracles of healing have a history that dates back thousands of years. In the Bible, the second Book of Kings contains a good example of this. Naaman, captain of the host of the king of Syria, was a successful soldier and an honorable man. However, all his success meant nothing once he contracted leprosy. His wife had a servant, a young Jewish girl, who suggested that Naaman visit Elisha, the famous healer-prophet in Samaria. The king of Syria agreed that he should go, and even offered to write a letter to the king of Israel.

The king of Israel was not pleased when he received this letter. After all, it could cause problems between the two countries if Elisha failed to cure Naaman. Elisha calmed the king down and suggested that it would be a politically good move for Naaman to visit.

Consequently, the great general arrived and was told by one of Elisha's servants to bathe seven times in the River Jordan. Naaman was extremely disappointed. He had expected something much more dramatic and miraculous than this. After all, the rivers of Syria were far superior to the River Jordan! Naaman turned around and began to return home. Fortunately, his servants suggested that he at least give the cure a try. It made sense after traveling all that way.

Naaman submitted to seven baths in the River Jordan. To his amazement, "his flesh came again like unto the flesh of a little child, and he was clean" (2 Kings 5:14). After this miraculous cure, Naaman returned to Elisha and offered him a generous payment. Naaman was astonished yet again when Elisha refused. He announced that from then on he would worship only the god of Israel.

Sadly, the story was not yet complete. Gehazi, one of Elisha's servants, felt that he should receive some reward himself. After all, he was a servant of the great healer. He ran after the Syrian general and virtually begged for a talent of silver and two changes of clothes. Naaman gave him two talents of silver as well as the two changes of clothes. When he returned to his master's house, Elisha knew what he had done. As a punishment, he passed on Naaman's leprosy to Gehazi, who "went out from his presence a leper as white as snow" (2 Kings 5:27).

Jesus was a renowned healer, as we have already seen. In addition to this, he was also an expert psychologist. When Jesus visited the Pool at Bethesda he came across a man who had been lame for thirty-eight years. Despite this incredible length of time, the man had made no real effort to enter the water to see if he could be healed. He had an excuse, of course. The first person to enter the pool after the waters had been disturbed by an angel was cured. This man claimed that he had no one to lift him into the water, and when he tried to get in, other people rushed in ahead of him. Obviously, he was gaining benefit by remaining ill, and enjoyed receiving sympathy and alms from others. It is common for people to actually enjoy being ill, and frequently this can provide them with an excuse for not facing up to the demands of life. These people may say that they want to be healed, and may try every method of healing they can think of, but because they are subconsciously gaining benefit from the illness, no healing method will work. Jesus was well aware of this, which is why he asked the man, "Whilt thou be made whole?" When he received a positive reply, Jesus told the man to take up his bed and walk (John 5:6).

The early Christian church placed a strong emphasis on healing. An example of this was when the apostle Peter instantly healed a man of the palsy. Aeneas had been bedridden for eight years. Peter said to him: "Aeneas, Jesus Christ maketh thee whole: arise, and make thy bed" (Acts 9:34).

Today, in famous healing centers such as Lourdes, the Catholic Church places most of its emphasis on restoring people's faith, rather than receiving healing miracles. In fact, Bernadette Soubirous, the young peasant girl, who saw the queen of heaven in a grotto in Lourdes in 1858, had little interest in the healing aspect of her experience. She was more concerned that people used the chapel to renew their faith.

Fourteen-year-old Bernadette was a quiet, obedient girl, the eldest of six children. One evening, she, her sister, and another girl were collecting firewood on the banks of the River Gave. Bernadette had fallen behind the other two. As she passed a small cave, Bernadette heard a strange sound, like a sudden breeze. However, there were no ripples on the water. She noticed a strange cloud of white and gold immediately in front of her. Out of this cloud stepped a beautiful young lady, glowing with a strange light. Her hair fell to her shoulders, and she was wearing a white gown with a blue sash around her waist. Bernadette immediately sank to her knees, and was still praying when the other two girls returned.

The look of rapture on her face was immediately obvious to her parents when the girls returned home. Despite swearing the other girls to secrecy, word quickly spread through the small village. Three days later, Bernadette returned to the river bank, and the lady appeared to her again. This time, curious villagers followed her, and they saw nothing. Not surprisingly, they teased her about her imaginary friend. Four days later, on February 18, Bernadette saw the lady again, and this time she spoke to her for the first time, telling her to return to the same spot every day for two weeks. The lady promised her great happiness in the next world.

The crowds grew larger every day as Bernadette returned to the cave and spoke to the lady that only she could see. Then, on February 25, the villagers saw Bernadette start digging into the earth with her hands. A small puddle appeared, and Bernadette drank from it. This puddle turned into a spring.

On one of her conversations with the lady, Bernadette asked who she was. The lady replied, "I am the Immaculate Conception."[1]

On March 2, with 1,600 people watching, the lady told Bernadette to build a chapel on the site. The village priest, Dominique Peyramale was not convinced. He called Bernadette a liar, and insisted the apparition name herself and also make a rosebush bloom in the next two days. 20,000 people arrived to see this miracle, but the rose bush failed to bloom and the apparition remained silent. However, a rumor spread through the crowd that Bernadette had restored the sight of a blind girl by breathing on her eyes.

It was now too late for the parish priests to stop the frenzy, and today five million people travel to Lourdes every year. Some 65,000 of them are hoping for a healing miracle. Sadly, these few weeks proved to be the high point of Bernadette's life. After some grueling questioning by church officials, Bernadette was sent away to a hospice school, and then became a nun. She died of tuberculosis, asthma, and other complications, in 1879, at the early age of thirty-five. Near the end of her life, she said poignantly, "I served the Virgin Mary as a simple broom. When she no longer had any use for me she put me back in my place behind the door."[2] Bernadette's response when asked about miracles that occurred at the shrine was: "I have been told that there have been miracles, but . . . I have not seen them."[3]

The International Medical Committee of Lourdes (IMCL) investigate all the sudden, unexplained cures, and consider just sixty-five of them to be "scientifically inexplicable." They prefer not to use the word "miracles." Some six thousand cases in which people claimed they had been miraculously cured have been rejected.4 The scientifically inexplicable cases are referred to the Vatican who decide whether or not a miracle has occurred.

One of the inexplicable cases concerned Pierre de Rudder, a Belgian, who broke his leg when a tree fell on him in 1867. Doctors wanted to amputate the injured limb, but Pierrer refused, despite the constant agonizing pain. Eventually, his employer arranged for him to make a pilgrimage to Lourdes. Dr. Van Hoestenberghe examined him in January 1875, just a few days before the pilgrimage. He wrote: "Rudder had an open wound at the top of the leg. In this wound one could see the two bones separated by a distance of three centimetres [about 1.2 inches]. There was no sign of healing . . . The lower part of the leg could be moved in all directions. The heel could be lifted in such a way as to fold the leg in the middle. It could be twisted, with the heel in front and the toes in back, all these movements being only restricted by the soft tissues."5

The shrine was crowded with people when Pierre arrived at Lourdes. Twice he tried to walk around the shrine, but was in too much pain to complete it. He sat down and prayed. He was overcome with emotion. After several minutes, he stood up and walked without hesitation to the statue of Our Lady of Lourdes where he knelt down. Suddenly, Pierre realized what he had done. He stood up again and walked around the shrine. His wife fainted when she saw him.

When Pierre arrived home, his younger son, who had never seen his father without crutches, refused to believe that it was him. Two physicians, including Dr. Van Hoestenberghe, examined him and found that he had been completely healed. His legs were the same length again, the bone was mended, and the wound had disappeared.

Pierre walked perfectly for the rest of his life. He died in 1898. The following year, Dr. Van Hoestenberghe exhumed the body and took a number of photographs to confirm the miracle. His report of this autopsy was published in the *Revue des Questions Scientifiques* in October 1899.[6]

Edeltraud Fulda is another example of someone who achieved a miraculous healing at Lourdes. In 1937, at the age of twenty-one, she was touring Italy as a professional dancer when she collapsed with a perforated ulcer. Two-thirds of her stomach had to be removed. A few months later, an abscess on a kidney had to be cut out. The following year a kidney had to be removed. None of this helped, and shortly afterward she was diagnosed with Addison's disease. The cure for this at the time was cortin, an extract taken from the adrenal glands of cattle. Edeltraud had to take this every day. Without it she collapsed. However, even with the help of cortin she remained seriously ill and was confined to a wheelchair.

In 1946, she decided to go to Lourdes. Edeltraud lived in Vienna, and it took four years of planning before she could take the trip. She arrived in Lourdes on August 12, 1950, and immediately bathed in the cold waters. She did not expect a cure until August 15, the Feast of the Assumption, but to her amazement, the cure was instantaneous. Three days later, she stopped taking cortin. When she returned home, her physician was amazed that she could survive without taking the drug. When he made further tests, he found that the Addison's disease was no longer present in her system. Even more amazing to him was the fact that the damage that had been done to her intestinal tract in her first operation had been completely cured.

Exactly one year later, Edeltraud led a pilgrimage of invalids to Lourdes. A delegation of thirty-three doctors saw her when she visited the medical bureau. They congratulated her on her cure, but refused to give her written confirmation of the miracle. This was disappointing. However, in 1954 a medical commission at Lourdes announced that her cure could not be explained on medical grounds. Finally, in March 1955, Cardinal Innitzer told her that the Catholic Church had pronounced her amazing recovery a miracle. Edeltraud Fulda recorded her story in a moving book called *And I Shall Be Healed: The Autobiography of a Woman Miraculously Cured at Lourdes*.[7]

In 1916, almost sixty years after Bernadette's experiences at Lourdes, three small children in Fatima, at that time a small village in the high country of central Portugal, saw an angel who told them to pray. Lucia dos Santos was ten-years-old. Her two cousins were younger. Francisco Marto was nine, and his sister Jacinta was seven. They saw this angel, who looked like a fifteen-year-old boy on three occasions. Several months later, on May 13, 1917 the three children were looking after the sheep when a flash of lightning made them drive the sheep downhill. A second flash of lightning revealed to the two girls a beautiful woman standing by an oak tree. She was wearing a white dress with a gold border.

Her head was covered in a white veil, but her face was visible. Around her neck was a gold cord.

Lucia asked the woman where she was from, and was told "heaven." The apparition said that she wanted to see the three children on the thirteenth of every month, and that after six months she would tell them who she was. Francisco was unable to see the woman at first, and suggested throwing a stone at it. The woman said that all three children would go to heaven, but Francisco would have to recite many rosaries first. He began praying, and was able to see the woman. The woman told them to pray for an end to the war, and then ascended into the sky and vanished.

The three children agreed to keep this strange occurrence a secret, but Jacinta was unable to do so. That night she told her mother what had happened, and very soon everyone in the village knew. The local priest, Father Ferreira, was shocked at the news, thinking that it was the work of the devil. Lucia's mother disbelieved the whole story, and accused the children of lying. Not even threats of a beating made the children change their story.

Fifty people returned to the site a month later to see if the Virgin Mother would return. They saw the three children kneeling in prayer beside the oak tree, and watched Lucia talking to someone they could not see. They heard an explosion when the apparition left, followed by a white cloud that sailed to the east. Some people claimed that the leaves of the oak trees all pointed east for some hours after the apparition had left.[8]

Lucia's mother beat her daughter for lying, but Lucia insisted they had seen the woman again. On July 13, some five thousand people heard Lucia speaking to the apparition. The woman again told the children to pray for an end to the war. Lucia asked for a miracle, to prove that they were not lying. The apparition promised this would occur on October 13. She also told them a secret that was never to be revealed.

The authorities began showing an interest in what was going on. On August 11, Arturo d'Oliveira Santos, subprefect of Ourém, came to Fatima to interview the children. When they denied lying, he took them to the Ourém town prison where he interrogated them separately. The children did not change a word of their story, even when he told them they'd be boiled in oil, and that the other two children were already dead. Santos treated the children heartlessly, because he thought the secret related to a plot to restore the monarchy. Finally, he was forced to release the children, but made sure he did not do this until after the thirteenth of the month.

Despite the absence of the children, eighteen-thousand people arrived to stand in front of the oak tree. Some of them thought that a clap of thunder created a flash of light that suffused everyone with rainbow colors.

The children were back in the fields looking after the sheep when the lady paid them a surprise visit on August 19. She told them not to miss any more meetings, and, as a result of their absence on the thirteenth, the miracle in October would not be as incredible as would otherwise have been the case.

Arturo d'Oliveira Santos had virtually abducted the children. News of this, plus what had occurred earlier, meant that some thirty-thousand people turned up on September 13. They all saw the sun dim and the stars come out, as a glowing circle of white light came down toward the tree. It disappeared as it reached the tree, and a rain of gleaming white petals began falling from the sky. While this was going on, the lady told the children that more prayer was needed, and that something terrible would happen if people did not change their ways. She again told them that a miracle would occur on October 13.

Not surprisingly, seventy-thousand pilgrims arrived the following month to witness the miracle. At noon, the children made their way through the kneeling crowd to the oak tree. Finally, the lady told the children that she was Our Lady of the Rosary. She wanted a chapel built on the site. When she spread her arms out wide, beams of pure light shone from them. Lucia called out, "Look up at the sun!"

It had been raining, but the clouds parted revealing a huge silver disc. It was the sun, but it was pale and people could look directly at it. The sun began whirling and dancing in a strange manner, tracing a spiral of circles in the sky, and gaining speed and momentum as it gyrated. Some witnesses said that streamers of flame emerged from the sun's rim. The spectators were terrified as the disc zigzagged toward them. It hovered above them for several minutes, instantly drying the drenched clothes of the weeping, praying, crying, fainting, and screaming pilgrims. After eight minutes it spiraled back into the sky and resumed its normal role as the sun. After three hours, the sun was once again too bright to look at.

The pilgrims left, all convinced that something extraordinary had occurred. Skeptics claimed it was mass hypnosis, but this was discounted when it emerged that people up to thirty miles away had witnessed the phenomenon. One of the witnesses was Avelino de Almeida, editor of a newspaper called *O Seculo*. He had written an article about the coming miracle in that morning's paper, in an attempt to attract attention to what he believed would be a dismal failure. On October 17, a lengthy account of what he had witnessed was printed in his paper, in which he described the sun's gyrations as a "macabre dance."9

After this extraordinary miracle, it took the Catholic church exactly thirteen years to accept the visions of the children as genuine visions of the Virgin Mary. The Bishop of Leiria announced this on October 13, 1930. However, the first national pilgrimage to Fatima occurred in 1927, and work on the basilica also began that year. It was consecrated in 1953. On May 13, 1967, one million people gathered at Fatima to hear Pope Paul VI say Mass and pray for world peace. On each side of the basilica are hospitals and retreat houses. Many miraculous cures have been reported, but the church has sought no publicity for them.

The Virgin Mary has appeared in a number of places, including Medjugorje. On June 24, 1981, four girls and two boys were playing on Podbrdo Hill near the village of Medjugorje. They were Ivanka and Vicka Invankovic, Mirjana and Ivan Dragicevic, Marija Pavlovic, and Jakov Colo. They ranged in age from seventeen to ten. They were startled by a sudden bright light surrounding a beautiful woman who was floating just above the ground. She was dark-haired, blue-eyed, and wearing a grey dress with a white mantle and veil. Circling above her head were twelve golden stars. She was holding a baby in her arms. She indicated that the children should come closer, but they ran away in fear. They returned the next day and the lady appeared again.

Ivanka asked her about her mother who had died two months earlier. The lady comforted her and told her to take care of her elderly grandmother. The lady told them that she was the Gospa, the Croatian Madonna. She said that she would keep on reappearing until she had told each of them ten secrets about the future. People must pray, repent, and fast, she told them.

As with Lourdes and Fatima, the word quickly spread. The authorities were unhappy with the situation, thinking that it might be a fascist plot. Other people thought the children were high on drugs. Fra Jozo Zovko, the Franciscan pastor of St. James Catholic Church in Medjugorje, did not know what to think, until one day, while praying, he heard a voice telling him to protect the children. He opened the doors of the church, just as the children appeared, saying that the police were chasing them to stop them from going up the hill. He invited them in, and almost every evening for the next ten years the Gospa appeared to the children in a small room in the church.

The Communist regime were unhappy about this, and recorded Fra Zovko's sermons, thinking that he was secretly behind the Gospa's depressing prophesies. Eventually, he was jailed for eighteen months.

However, the fame of Medjugorje could not be stopped. Twenty million people made a pilgrimage to Medjugorje in the following ten years. People seeking a cure crawled on hands and knees to the top of Mount Krizevac, the hill of the cross. At least three hundred cures have been claimed, including a well-documented one of a Scottish nurse called Heather Duncan, who crawled up the mountain with a crushed spine. She managed to walk down again, and is still walking, even though, as she says: "My X-rays show I shouldn't be able to walk."[10]

Naturally, as well as healing centers, there are many gifted people around the world who have the ability to heal others. Many of these healings can only be described as miraculous.

One of the most famous of these healers was the Brazilian, José Pedro de Freitas (1918–1971), better known as Arigó, the psychic surgeon. He performed thousands of diagnoses and operations while in a trance state. He claimed that a Dr. Adolphus Fritz, a German doctor who died in Estonia in 1918, told him what to do.

While still at school, Arigó occasionally experienced strange hallucinations, in which he saw a brilliant light and heard someone speaking in a strange language. By the time he was in his middle twenties, he began experiencing vivid dreams, in which a doctor spoke to a group of doctors and nurses in the strange language that he first heard in his teenage hallucinations. In time, the man told Arigó that he was Dr. Adolphus Fritz, and that he had died during the First World War. Because he knew Arigó was honest and caring, he wanted him to carry on the work he had been unable to finish. Always, after these dreams, Arigó suffered a severe headache.

In 1950, several years after these nightmares began, Arigó was invited to attend a political rally by Lúcio Bittencourt, one of the campaigners. At the time Bittencourt was seriously ill with lung cancer, and his doctors had recommended that he go to the United States for an operation. Arigó was unaware of this. However, as Bittencourt was about to go to sleep one night, the door to his hotel room opened and Arigó walked in. His eyes seemed glazed, and he was carrying a razor. Speaking with a guttural German accent, he told Bittencourt that it was an emergency, and he had to operate. Bittencourt lost consciousness and had no memory of the operation. However, when he came to, his pajama top was slashed and bloodstained. He went to Arigó's room. Arigó had no memory of the operation and denied all knowledge of it. Bittencourt returned to Río de Janeiro and saw his doctor. The doctor assumed that Bittencourt had had an operation in the United States, and told him that the tumor had been removed by a technique that he was not familiar with. Bittencourt told the doctor what had occurred, and soon the newspapers were telling everyone about the miracle.

For the next six years Arigó saw up to three hundred patients a day. However, in 1956 the Catholic Church and the medical establishment had him charged with practicing medicine without a license, even though he never charged anyone for his healing work. Arigó was sentenced to eighteen months in jail, although this was later reduced to eight months.

Arigó stopped practicing for a while, but when the headaches began again, he resumed his healing work. In 1958, President Kubitschek gave him a presidential pardon. However, by 1961, Kubitschek was out of office, and Arigó's opponents began pressing for more legal action.

In 1963, Arigó received national publicity again when he removed a tumor from the arm of an American investigator, Dr. Andrija Puharich. However, this was not enough to stop his opponents, and in November 1964, he was sentenced to sixteen months in jail.

In 1968, Dr. Andrija Puharich returned with a fellow researcher and watched him treat a thousand patients. Without touching them, and spending less than a minute with each patient, Arigó diagnosed and recommended the correct treatment for each one. Afterwards, Dr. Puharich said: "we did not find [one] in which Arigó was at fault."[11] This was an amazing feat when one remembers that Arigó was an uneducated, former miner. The nickname "Arigó," which he was given as a child, can be loosely translated as "country bumpkin." Arigó was unable to explain his extraordinary talent, but credited Jesus and Dr. Adolphus Fritz. Sadly, Arigó died in a car accident in 1971, after telling several people that they would not see him again. 20,000 mourners attended his funeral.[12]

Arigó needed to see his patients. Edgar Cayce (1877–1945) did not. As long as he had the patient's name and address, he could go into a trance, and give a diagnosis and suggested course of treatment. This is known as absent healing. Edgar Cayce was also able to provide details of his patients' past lives.

Absent healing is also regularly performed by prayer. One well-documented case concerned Matthew Simpson (1811–1884), a bishop in the Methodist Episcopal Church. A group of ministers were at a conference in Mount Vernon, Ohio, and were told that

Bishop Simpson was close to death in a hospital bed in Pittsburgh. The clergymen immediately prayed for the bishop, asking that his life be spared. One of them was Thomas Bowman, also a bishop in the same church. He recalled that after the first few sentences of the prayer, his mind became totally at ease, as he knew that his brother bishop would be saved. Once the prayer was over, he expressed his views to the others, and thirty of them said they had experienced the same feeling that the bishop would be saved. It was several months before Thomas Bowman saw Bishop Simpson, fit and well again. Bishop Simpson said that he had no idea what had happened, but that his doctor had declared it a miracle. The bishop had been at the point of death, but somehow made a startling improvement at the exact time that the ministers were praying for him.[13]

In recent years, a number of people have studied miracle cures. One of these was the late Brendan O'Regan, formerly vice-president for research at the Institute of Noetic Sciences at Sausalito, California. He found that people who experienced sudden, dramatic cures were not demanding of a cure. They had an attitude of acceptance and gratitude, despite their illness. They could not explain the miracle cure, either, saying that it "just happened."[14] This seems to indicate that the people who demand a miracle cure are the ones least likely to receive it, while others who relax, and "go with the flow" are more likely to receive a cure.

Most of the healings we have mentioned here have involved taking a pilgrimage to a healing center, or have required an especially gifted person to manifest the healing energies. Fortunately, it is possible for you to create miracles in your own life without the necessity of taking a long trip or seeking out a special person. We will start on this in the next chapter.

Three

Miracles in
Your Own Life

SEVERAL YEARS AGO, a
friend of mine was driving down a freeway late at
night. He was in the center of three lanes, with
cars on either side of him. As they rounded a
corner, he saw a car heading directly toward the
car in the fast lane. As Gareth was trapped
between the cars on either side, all he could do
was put on his brakes to slow down. The cars
on either side of him did the same. As they did
this, the approaching car swerved in front of
Gareth. Gareth's car tipped the corner of this car
as it ploughed into the car in the slow lane.

The accident killed the driver of the car that
was going the wrong way. Because of this, it
was impossible to determine how he had managed to end up on the wrong side of the freeway. The family in the car he hit were bruised,

but not badly hurt. Gareth was shaken, but sustained no injuries. When Gareth told me about this incident, he said that it was a miracle that he had not been hurt or killed. However, was this a miracle, luck, or simply chance? Gareth's account of the incident made me wonder.

"When I saw the car coming towards us, I had time to think what a crazy idiot the driver was. I felt sorry for the car that he was heading towards, and put on my brakes, hoping that that car might be able to move into my lane. There wasn't time for that, of course. Anyway, when the car swerved in front of me, I didn't panic. I remained totally calm. I knew that I would survive the accident that was about to happen. You could almost say I was detached from the outcome. When the corners of our cars touched, I was able to concentrate on my steering, so I didn't plough into the side of the other cars. I heard and saw him crash into the other car, and then was able to stop to see what help I could offer. I remained completely calm, until the paramedics arrived. Only then did I go into shock."

Gareth's feelings of detachment, almost as if he was watching the accident happening to someone else, is a common factor in this sort of incident. Until this accident, Gareth had no faith, but immediately afterward he began exploring the spiritual side of his makeup. People with a faith often feel this sense of detachment when faced with a difficult situation, such as an accident. They realize that they are in the hands of the divine, and need not be concerned. In a sense, these people are being looked after by a power greater than themselves, and this appears to ensure their survival.

Consequently, I felt that Gareth's survival was more than mere chance. In a difficult situation, in which most other people would have panicked, he remained calm, unruffled, detached and observant. This experience may not be a miracle in the usual sense of the word, but it most certainly was a miracle to Gareth.

Of course, there is no way of knowing how we would act in a similar situation. However, we can learn the necessary qualities in advance, so that if we are faced with a potentially disastrous situation, we are more likely to act in a way that will encourage a personal miracle to occur.

The necessary qualities are: contentment, serendipity, intuition, universal love, faith, and a willingness to make any necessary changes in our attitude toward life.

Contentment

You must appreciate what you already have. Many people are never happy in the present. They spend most of their time dwelling on the past, or worrying about the future. Obviously, it is important to make plans for the future, and it is pleasant to relive moments from the past. However, the here and now is all that we have. If you spend most of your time thinking about past mistakes or worrying about the future, you end up missing out on life in the here and now.

An acquaintance of mine is always planning to be happy when a certain thing occurs. "I'll be happy when I get a new car," he might say. Or, "When I get promoted, I'll be happy." There is no need to wait until something occurs to be happy. Live in the present, and be happy now. Many years ago, Tai L'au, a good friend and mentor, told me, "If you want to be happy, be happy." It was deceptively simple, but extremely powerful advice.

Contentment is not determined by the amount of money you have, the state of your health, or the number of friends you have. It is a state of mind in which you appreciate and enjoy the present moment.

There is no guarantee that any of us will be here tomorrow. Today is all we have. Make the most of every day. Nurture yourself. Appreciate your good qualities, and all the blessings in your life. Someone told me once that whenever he had trouble falling to sleep at night, he would mentally run through everything he could think of to be grateful for. It would be hard to remain discontented for long, if you made that a daily practice.

Serendipity

Dictionaries define serendipity as the ability to make fortunate discoveries by accident. I would extend that definition slightly. If you expect fortunate discoveries to occur, they will. They may even appear to be happy accidents, but in reality, they will occur because you have subconsciously sent out the correct conditions for them to occur.

If you lead your life in the expectation that good things will happen to you, you somehow become a magnet that will attract good things to you. This is because we become what we think about. We also receive what we expect to receive. People who live their lives this way experience serendipitous happenings on a regular basis. Naturally, if you open yourself up to the possibility of good things occurring unexpectedly all the time, you are also opening yourself up to the possibility of creating miracles in your own life.

The word "serendipity" was coined by the British author, Horace Walpole (1717–1797). He wrote a fairy story called *The Three Princes of Serendip*, which was about three boys who constantly made discoveries by happy accident.

Intuition

Everybody has a small, quiet voice inside themselves that guides, warns, and counsels. It is sometimes known as a hunch or "gut feeling." Many people ignore it. They either fail to hear it, or believe their difficulties can only be surmounted with thought. Other people use it some of the time. They are the ones who say, "I knew I shouldn't have done that." Hopefully, in time they will learn to heed their quiet, internal voice more often, and develop their intuition. Naturally, intuitive people listen to it all the time. In my own life, I know that many of the mistakes I have made would not have happened if I had acted on my intuition, rather than logic.

Universal Love

Universal love is an impartial love for all of humanity. It is a love that comes from the heart and soul, and does not seek any return. However, the rewards are incredible. It enables you to see the good in all, and you will recognize the God in everyone you meet. When you live your life with a sense of love, empathy, and concern for all living creatures you open yourself to many blessings. For instance, everyone you meet will sense your love, and will respond by sending love back to you. This will have an effect on every area of your life. The more love you send out, the more you will receive back in return.

Faith

Faith refers to your connection with the divine. The closer you become to this source, the more personal power you will possess. Each time you do something that goes against your personal moral or ethical standards, the weaker the connection becomes.

The word "faith" has religious overtones, but it is not necessary to belong to any religion to have a faith. Faith can be a belief in anything, such as ethical standards or a code of conduct. If you believe that good will always prevail, for instance, you will see this manifest in your own life, as your faith will have attracted it to you. Likewise, if you believe that miracles can occur, you will experience the miraculous in your own life.

Willingness to Change

P. D. Ouspensky (1878–1947), the Russian philosopher and mystic, wrote a powerful, but little-known, novel called *Strange Life of Ivan Osokin*.[1] Ivan was a young man who was on the brink of suicide. He had failed at everything he had attempted and had just been rejected by the woman he loved. He visited a wise magician to complain about the bleakness of his life. He claimed that if only he could live his life over again, everything would be different. Instead of receiving sympathy, the magician disagreed, and told Ivan that he would repeat all the same mistakes again. Ivan was annoyed and did not believe what the magician said. He asked if he could have the chance to relive at least part of his life. The magician sent Ivan back twelve years, and he was astonished to find himself reliving the exact same experiences in the same depressing manner as before. Despite everything he tried to do, he was unable to change the direction of his life. Ivan returned to the magician to ask him how this could be possible. The magician told him that for his life to be different, he had to be different. His entire inner life had to change, and this took a great deal of hard work and effort. However, once he did this, he would cease being a loser, and achieve the success he craved.

You can change your life if you want to. The first step toward self-transformation is the desire to become a different person. You then need to look at yourself honestly, seek advice, if necessary, and be persistent. It takes time, alertness, discipline and hard work.

Can you see how you would remain calm, detached and accepting in a difficult situation, such as an accident, once you have developed these traits? When you consciously develop these qualities you open yourself up to the possibility of experiencing miracles in your own life.

Whenever I give talks on the subject of miracles, I can almost guarantee that someone will ask about the element of luck, and whether or not someone can experience a miracle by some lucky chance. I reply that luck can play a part in anything, including miracles, and by working on the five qualities discussed in this chapter, we are encouraging luck to be on our side. Luck can be defined as a force, or combination of circumstances, that operates for good or ill in someone's life. Good luck supposedly occurs as a result of chance, but I believe that there is much more to it than this. If we deliberately foster the qualities we desire, we are much more likely to receive the results we want (good luck), and less likely to experience bad luck. We cannot discard the concept of luck entirely, but we can certainly put the odds on our side.

Winston Churchill did this extremely effectively all the way through life. This enabled him to miraculously produce a magician to entertain the troops during the Boer War. Winston Churchill was working as a war correspondent at the time, and parlayed this feat into a scoop for his newspaper. This looks like two miracles, but Winston Churchill was simply using his lifelong skills of observation, keenness, and enthusiasm. Not for nothing was Churchill referred to as "that lucky devil, Churchill."

In this instance, Winston Churchill and several other war correspondents had ridden past a line of Boer prisoners and seen one of them expertly knotting a bandage on his left arm with his right hand. The other correspondents rode past, but Churchill's curiosity was aroused. He got off his horse and spoke to the prisoner, who happened to speak good English. He told Churchill that he was a German, who normally made his living performing sleight-of-hand in music halls.

A day or two later, Churchill heard the British commander talking about the low morale of his bored men. Churchill immediately suggested that a professional magic show would motivate and entertain everyone. To everyone's amazement, he was able to produce the magician, who did an excellent show. To show his appreciation and gratitude, the general gave Churchill a previously unknown piece of news that gave him, yet again, a scoop.[2]

The amazingly rapid growth of eBay is another apparent miracle. However, it is another example of someone who was mentally prepared to accept an opportunity when it presented itself. Pierre Omidyar, a French-born technology student, had bought a laser pointer to entertain his cat. The cat enjoyed chasing the red beam around the living room. Unfortunately, after a few days the pointer broke. Rather than returning it to the store, Pierre thought it would be fun to see if he could sell it on Auctionweb, a website that he had set up in 1995. He listed it as a "broken laser pointer" and was surprised when someone bought it for $14.00. Puzzled by this, Pierre e-mailed the purchaser to find out why he had bought it. The man replied that he liked fixing things.

This was all the encouragement that Pierre needed. Auctionweb quickly transformed itself into eBay, and now sells virtually anything you could think of. eBay is the biggest car lot in America, selling an SUV every thirty seconds. One computer game is sold every eight seconds. More than 150,000 people have become full-time traders on eBay, some selling more than $150,000 worth of merchandise every month. Pierre's alertness to opportunity, willingness to work hard, and good management skills took the broken laser pointer and created one of the most successful businesses on the Internet. Pierre is now a multibillionaire, a miracle by any standards.[3]

Winston Churchill and Pierre Omidyar were both alert to opportunities and recognized them when they occurred. These are qualities that everyone has. The difference is that they seized the opportunity and made it work for them. Only you can decide if you are going to seize the right opportunity when it comes your way. If you do, you will be able to create apparent miracles. Then people will start saying: "that lucky devil, (your name)."

Now that you know the necessary qualities that you need to acquire, we can look at the methods of the ancient Kahunas in Hawaii. They had a number of expert techniques that they used to work miracles. Their principles are just as effective today as they ever have been, and clearly show some of the essential qualities necessary for miracles to occur.

Four

Miracles and
the Hunas

Long before Captain
James Cook discovered the Hawaiian Islands in
1778, the local inhabitants had a well-developed
religious system called *Huna*. The word Huna
means "secret" in Hawaiian. The leaders of this
religion were Kahunas ("keepers of the secret").
The Kahunas were priests, healers, prophets,
counselors, and experts on all aspects of life in
the islands.

Huna is a science, a philosophy, and a religion. It is a science because it involves the physical world, and its techniques are repeatable. It is
a philosophy of life, with a strong emphasis on
moral and ethical behavior. It is a religion because
it encourages people to grow spiritually, and find
God within themselves. Many people consider it
to be magic, too, as it deals with invisible forces
and produces incredible results.

This idyllic way of life changed forever thirty-five years after Captain Cook's visit when Christian missionaries arrived. They thought the inhabitants were ignorant savages who had to be converted to Christianity. To be fair, the missionaries did not speak the local language and were probably not aware of Huna. The locals, decimated by Western illnesses, and believing the missionaries to be their benefactors, gradually lost touch with their old religion.

Fortunately, Dr. William Tufts Brigham, curator of the Bishop Museum in Honolulu, began studying and researching Huna in the late nineteenth century. He witnessed fire-walking, and the Kahuna methods of healing. He even witnessed a miracle, when a young man who had drowned sixteen hours earlier was brought back to life using Huna magic.[1]

Max Freedom Long (1890–1971) did more than anyone to promote interest in Huna. In 1917, he left college in California, and accepted a position as a teacher at a tiny school on a sugar plantation in Hawaii. He had plenty of free time to explore, meditate, study, and talk with the native people. He heard many stories about the Kahunas, fire-walking, and miracle healings, but found that whenever he tried to gain further information his sources stopped talking. Max Freedom Long was an outsider, and the people would not confide in him. In 1919 he approached Dr. Brigham to see what scientific research had been done on the subject. The two men became friends, and Max Freedom Long was given access to all the information stored at the Bishop Museum.

Dr. Brigham had spent forty years studying the subject and was overjoyed to find someone who would carry on with his research. Dr. Brigham emphasized that there had to be three factors involved in Huna. First, there had to be some form of consciousness that directed the magic. Second, some form of force had to be used to make it work, and third, there had to be a substance of some sort, visible or invisible, that the force could work within. Finding any one of these, he told Max, could lead on to finding the others.[2]

Max Freedom Long studied with Dr. Brigham until the old man died in 1926. Max continued with his research, but five years later, in 1931, was forced to admit defeat. He returned to California where he found work managing a camera shop. However, his quest was still at the back of his mind.

One night, in 1935, Max suddenly woke up with an awareness that the Kahunas must have had names for the various elements in Huna. Without definite names, it would have been impossible for them to pass their knowledge down from generation to generation. With great excitement, Max began studying the chants and prayers of the hunas in an attempt to discover what had been eluding him for all these years.

By the end of the year, Max had managed to discover two of the three missing elements. However, it took another six years of hard work to identify the final one. The consciousness was called *aumakua* (Higher Self), the necessary force was called *mana* (life force, ch'i, prana, energy), and the invisible substance that the force acted in and through was *aka* (etheric substance, or shadow of a person).

It was hard enough to discover all of this. Getting this knowledge out to the world was also difficult. Max Freedom Long's first book on the subject, *Recovering the Ancient Magic*, had been printed and was waiting to be bound, when the printer's premises were destroyed by a bomb during the German blitz of London in the Second World War. Fortunately, he had more success with his later books, all of which are still in print.

The Kahunas had, in fact, created a perfect psychological system. They believed that we consist of three selves, which Max Freedom Long, for the sake of convenience, called the Low Self, the Middle Self, and the High Self. The Kahunas called them *unihipili, uhane,* and *aumakua.* Each of these selves has an invisible body made of an etheric substance that is much finer than physical matter. The Kahunas called these bodies *kino-aka.* These three bodies are totally interconnected with each other, and with the physical body they serve. They can be visualized as Russian nesting dolls, with the High Self being the outermost doll, containing the medium sized Middle Self, which also contains inside it the slightly smaller Low Self. However, unlike the nesting dolls, each kino-aka body totally interconnects with the others. In practice, most of the time, the middle and low selves remain closely intertwined with the physical body, while the High Self remains in its shadowy body above the physical body.

Mana

The three selves need nourishment to enable them to work properly. The Low Self uses mana, which at its most basic is air.

Without air, we would be dead in just a few minutes. Consequently, air is sometimes referred to as the universal life force, vital energy, or food of life. The Middle Self needs mana-mana, which is created from mana, and supplied by the Low Self. It is a stronger, more vital form of energy. The High Self uses mana-loa, which is the highest form of energy. It is mana-loa that can effect miracles, such as instantaneous healings.

The Kahunas recognized that as air was the essence of life, offerings of mana (air) to the High Self (the godhead) was a worthwhile gift, similar in many ways to a sacrificial offering. Mana is breathed in by the Middle Self, transformed by the Low Self, and then sent to the High Self where it can be used to effect miracles.

The Low Self (Unihipili)

The Low Self corresponds to our subconscious mind and is symbolically located in the solar plexus. It is referred to as the Low Self purely because of its symbolic placement in the body. It is just as important as the other selves. All feelings and emotions are stored in the Low Self. The Low Self is also where all memories are stored. Every feeling you have ever experienced is stored in your Low Self.

The Middle Self (Uhane)

The Middle Self is located on the left side of the head and corresponds to our conscious mind. Everything our conscious mind thinks about is fed to the Low Self, which then acts on it. In other words, thinking takes place in the Middle Self, while feeling occurs in the Low Self.

The High Self (Aumakua)

The High Self is located approximately five feet above our heads, and corresponds to our superconscious mind. It is our spiritual self. It is attached to the right side of our heads by a golden cord. It can be construed as being our guardian angel, the god within us, or as part of the universal life force that is in all living things. The Kahunas called it "The Great Parent," as it can be visualized as a spiritual mother or father. When the Kahunas prayed, they addressed their prayers to their high selves, rather than to one supreme God. This means, of course, that they prayed to the part of themselves that was already a god. Every High Self is in contact with every other High Self, demonstrating the interconnectedness between all living things. The Great Poe Aumakua means "the family of high selves." When we use the methods of the Kahunas we make use of this part of us that is already a god. As gods, we can achieve anything, even miracles.

Aka

The three bodies are made up of an etheric substance known as aka. This etheric substance is sticky. It attaches itself to everything it touches, creating a network of fine threads connecting it to everything it has seen or touched. Communication takes place along each of these threads, enabling us to send thoughts or energies to others. The densest body is that of the Low Self, and people who can see auras see this body as the etheric body.

Aka Cord

The three selves are also joined by a cord of this etheric sub-stance, known as the aka cord. This enables mana to be trans-formed and sent from the Low Self to the other selves.

All three bodies are an integral part of you. To be happy, con-tented, successful and healthy, all three selves have to be in bal-ance. A blockage between two selves creates dis-ease. It prevents the free flow of mana energy and holds you back from being all that you can be. Your emotions are the most likely cause of any blockages. Negative thinking, feelings of inferiority, guilt, greed, envy, and hatred all affect our ability to progress in this lifetime. Fortunately, it is possible to use the Kahuna techniques to elimi-nate all negativity and lead a rich, fulfilled life. That may seem like a miracle, but as you will see shortly, it is not hard to do.

The Kahuna Ritual

The Kahuna ritual, sometimes known as the *Ha Rite,* involves using your Middle Self to decide exactly what it is that you desire. Once you have done that, the desire is mixed with sufficient mana and sent to the Low Self, which transforms the mana and sends it to the High Self where the desire will be acted upon. There is no need to concern yourself with how the High Self will achieve this. It may not happen exactly the way you thought it would, but it will happen. Faith and repetition is essential.

The desire needs to be as specific as possible. Do not ask for a specific sum of money, for instance, unless you need that amount of money for some purpose. Money is an essential part of life, of course, even though it is only a means of exchange. Think about what you want the money for, and ask for that. You might need enough money to make a down payment on a house. You might want extra money for a few luxuries. You might want money to help a friend who needs support. It makes no difference what you want the money for, but the intent has to be totally clear in your mind.

If you are seeking a partner, think about the qualities you would like this person to possess. If you are looking for a better job, think about what you would like to be doing. If you want to go on vacation, think about the place you wish to visit, and also consider the type of accommodation you desire, and everything else that would ensure you enjoy a memorable vacation.

Once you have the desire clear in your mind, you are ready to start. Make sure that you will be undisturbed, and tell no one what you are doing. You can perform the rite anywhere, at any time. However, you might have a favorite place in which to perform it. There might be a specific room or area in your home that you can use for this purpose. A sacred place in your home where you perform spiritual or magical work, would be perfect for the Kahuna rituals. If you wish, decorate the room with candles, flowers, incense, and anything else that feels right. You want the room to feel warm, inviting and sacred.

Eight Steps to a Miracle

1. Relax in a comfortable chair for a few minutes. Think about your desire. Imagine that you already have it, and think how much better your life is now that your request has been granted. Take a few deep breaths and allow the muscles of your body to relax as you exhale.

2. Once you feel completely relaxed, get up, and stand with your feet about eighteen inches apart. If possible, do this in front of an open window, to ensure that the mana you inhale will be the very best that you can provide. Focus on your breathing, and remember that each breath you take is full of life-sustaining energy. This is the mana that is required to feed your three selves.

3. When you feel ready, take four slow, deep breaths. Inhale as much air as possible, and hold it for a few seconds before exhaling slowly. As you do this, remind yourself that you are inhaling an abundance of beneficial mana that will provide a bountiful offering to your High Self. You might like to mentally picture the mana filling up your entire body and flowing out from the top of your head, as if you were a container full of water. Water is a symbol of energy and life to the Kahunas. You have now sent the mana down to your Low Self. The next part of the exercise is to send it up to your High Self. (Repeat this stage if you feel you are not yet full of mana.)

4. Visualize a circle of radiant, white light in the region of your solar plexus. As you picture it, imagine this white light suddenly shooting like a rocket upwards through your chest, neck and head, and up to your High Self. Picture it as a large circle of vibrant energy above your head. This is your offering of mana, that has been transformed into mana-loa by your Low Self, and has now been given to your High Self.

5. Gaze at the circle of energy and see your desire clearly imprinted on it. Visualize this as clearly as you can. This stage is the key part of the entire ritual. It is imperative that you know exactly what you want, and can picture it clearly inside the circle of energy above your head. See it vividly and with as much detail as possible. If you are seeking a new car, for instance, picture the model, color, and every other distinguishing feature of the specific car that you desire. Picture your desire in your mind for as long as you can. Believe with every fiber of your being that you already have whatever it is you are asking for.

6. Say out loud, with all the force and energy you can muster : "I desire (whatever it happens to be). This request harms no one. I am drawing my request to me NOW!" Repeat this request three times, using the same words each time.

7. Wait a few seconds, and then say quietly: "Thank you Great Father (or Great Mother, Great Parent, Universal Consciousness, or God) for all the blessings in my life. I appreciate everything you do for me. Thank you."

8. Sit down and relax for a few minutes before carrying on with your day. There is no need to give your request any more thought. You have passed it on to your High Self and the matter will be taken care of for you.

Once you have completed this ritual you will feel full of energy and joie de vivre. Some people have told me that it is just like a natural high. It is important that you feel this energy and excitement afterwards, as it means that your request has been successfully sent and received.

Naturally, you will be impatient, and will want quick results. Sometimes this occurs. Miraculous healings are often instantaneous. However, most requests take time to appear. Remember that your High Self does not somehow drop your request into your lap. However, it will influence the universal forces to arrange a way for you to receive your request. You will need to be alert for the right opportunity to arrive. Once you find it, you will probably have to work hard to achieve your goal.

Repeat the ritual at least once a day, and preferably twice a day, until your request has been provided. Remember that your High Self wants to help and serve you. It is your partner, your guardian angel. Your High Self has a vested interest in helping you become all you can be. With your High Self on your side, success is guaranteed. Trust your High Self, no matter how long it takes to grant your request, and you will receive the results you desire.

Jennifer's Experience

I met Jennifer at a hypnotherapy convention I attended some years ago. During the course of a presentation on the pendulum, I talked about the Kahuna ritual, and then had all the attendees go through the ritual with the goal of being more successful in their practices. Jennifer came and spoke to me afterwards. She was twenty-seven years old, and had been studying hypnotherapy as an interest. She had no intention of setting up her own practice. She worked as a sales representative for a printing company, and wanted to know if she could use the ritual to progress and become a sales manager. I gave her a few suggestions, and promptly forgot all about the conversation.

Two months later, I received a phone call from Jennifer. She had been performing the ritual every day. After several weeks there had been no changes, and she was starting to doubt that anything would happen. Strangely, out of the blue she received two offers on the same day. Both corporations wanted to employ her as a sales manager. Neither position had been advertised. Somehow the universe had sent two excellent opportunities to her.

"Which one did you accept?" I asked.

"I was so confused, I didn't know what to do," Jennifer said. "But then I remembered your talk on the pendulum. I attached my wedding ring to a piece of cotton, and asked it to tell me which one to choose. It's the position that's offering slightly less starting pay, but there's the opportunity to buy into the company, so long term it looks very promising. I'm starting on Monday!"

Jennifer's experience is an interesting one, as her High Self presented her with two opportunities. She felt this was a true miracle, as she had not applied for either position, yet both had been offered to her as a result of practicing the Huna ritual.

The Kahunas and Health

The Kahunas believe that health problems are caused by disharmony with the High Self. Vibrant health occurs only when all three selves are balanced and working in harmony with each other. Many health problems are related to negative thinking. When the Middle Self keeps feeding the Low Self with negative thoughts, filling it with anger, hatred and bitterness, it is not surprising that health problems can result. All of this negativity blocks the aka connection between the Low Self and the High Self, creating an imbalance, which then reveals itself in ill health. Physical problems in the body often have emotional causes. An inability to express one's emotional needs, for example, may well lead to problems with the throat. Likewise, failure to establish close loving relationships can lead to problems with the heart.

The Low Self feels, rather than thinks. Consequently, it accepts uncritically everything that is given to it. It is not the fault of the Low Self if you become unwell. It is simply doing what it is programmed to do, and the remedy is to constantly fill it with positive thoughts and emotions.

You have between fifty and sixty thousand thoughts a day. If you are like most people, you will seldom take charge of your thinking, which means that you have no idea how many thoughts are positive and how many are negative. From now on, resolve to stay on top of your thinking. Whenever you find yourself thinking negative thoughts, and everyone does, simply turn the thought into a positive one. There is no need to berate yourself when you catch yourself thinking negatively. Stop thinking the negative thoughts, and focus on something positive. It is a constant battle, but the rewards are tremendous.

Feelings of hurt and guilt can also cause health problems. The basic law of Huna is that you hurt no one. If you deliberately hurt someone else, you are likely to feel guilty. You should not allow yourself to feel guilty if you accidentally hurt someone. However, you should always do whatever you can to make amends, regardless of whether the hurt was deliberate or accidental.

You should also do what you can to avoid being hurt by others. If someone hurts you in any way, tell the person what he or she has done. Express your feelings. It is better to handle the situation right away, rather than letting it grow and fester in your mind.

There is a simple experiment you can do to see how much unwanted baggage you are carrying around with you. It is called Working with the Three Selves.

Working with the Three Selves Ritual

1. Sit down in a comfortable chair and take a few deep breaths. Consciously relax all of the muscles in your body. I usually do this by relaxing the muscles in the toes of my left foot. I allow the relaxation to drift from my toes into my foot, until it feels totally relaxed. I then do the same with my right foot. When both feet are completely relaxed, I allow the relaxation to drift up both legs, until my calves, knees and thighs feel totally relaxed. I then allow the relaxation to spread into my stomach and up into my chest. After this I relax the muscles in both shoulders, and then focus on my left arm, allowing it to completely relax, before doing the same with my right arm. I then relax the muscles in my neck, before allowing the relaxation to spread over my face and up to the top of my head. Finally, I mentally scan my entire body to make sure that every part is as relaxed as possible. Once you have done this and feel totally relaxed, you can start communicating with your three selves.

2. Focus on your solar plexus and start thinking about your Low Self. Think about the wonderful job it does for you, and silently thank it. Give thanks for its ability to remember

everything, for its wisdom, and ability to carry out the demands of your Middle Self. Thank it also for its ability to store and handle emotions. We all like to be thanked every now and again, and your three selves are no exception. However, the thanking has to be done genuinely. There is no point in spouting words that mean nothing to you, as each of your three selves will instantly recognize any insincerity.

3. Ask your Low Self to reveal the unwanted baggage you are carrying around. You may receive a clear picture of it in your mind. You may feel a physical sensation in your solar plexus. You may experience a sense of knowing what it is.

4. Ask your Low Self to give you some idea as to what your life would be like without these unwanted feelings and emotions. Again, you may experience this in different ways. It may be a sense of lightness, a warm sensation in your stomach, or a feeling of overpowering joy.

5. Thank your Low Self for revealing the baggage to you. Express your love to your Low Self.

6. Direct your attention to your Middle Self on the left side of your head. Thank your Middle Self for working tirelessly on your behalf every day. Thank it for its qualities of thinking and synthesizing information. Thank it for its will power, its strength, its ability to initiate and follow through.

7. Ask your Middle Self if the aka cord between it and your Low Self are clear. If this channel is blocked, ask what needs to be done to clear it. Ask your Middle Self to help you feed it only good, positive thoughts, so that only positive messages are sent to your Low Self.

8. Express your love to your Middle Self.

9. Focus your attention on your High Self. Visualize it five feet above you, attached to your head by a beautiful golden cord.

Experience the love that is constantly showered on you by your High Self.

10. Thank your High Self for watching over you, and for its willingness to help any time you ask for it. Ask your High Self for any insights it can offer to help you at this time. Pause for a couple of minutes, enjoying this intimate contact with your High Self. Thank your High Self again.

11. Take three slow deep breaths. Gradually allow yourself to become familiar with your surroundings, and when you feel ready, get up and continue with your day.

You will find this a good exercise to do on a regular basis. The better you get to know your three selves, the better your life will become. You will be able to ask them questions about any aspect of your life, and will always receive useful answers, as they have your best interests in mind all the time. You might do this exercise because you have a specific question to ask, and the input of your three selves will help you make the right decision. You may also choose to do this exercise to express your thanks and love to your three selves for constantly looking after you.

Kahuna Ritual for Vitality

When you are full of vitality and energy, you feel as if you can do anything. Sadly, many people seldom experience this state. They drag themselves through life, constantly listless and lacking in energy. Naturally, you need sufficient rest, but after a good night's sleep you should have plenty of energy to enable you to handle everything the day has to offer. Although you may not realize it, you possess limitless power, and can achieve anything you set your mind on. This Kahuna ritual will fill you with energy, enthusiasm, vitality, and power any time you need it.

1. Sit down in a comfortable chair and relax your body.

2. When you feel ready, get up. Stand with your feet twelve to eighteen inches apart.

3. Take four slow, deep breaths, holding each breath for a few seconds before exhaling. With each breath imagine that you are filling yourself to overflowing with bountiful mana.

4. After four breaths, mentally picture yourself full of mana. You might want to close your eyes to help visualize this. Take another deep breath and, in your mind, see this additional mana flowing out from the top of your head. I like to visualize this as a constant stream of water, overflowing and spilling out from the top of my head. This mana is pure energy, and when I see it spilling out from the top of my head, I know that I am overflowing with energy, and am ready for anything. As this mana is also a healing balm, this is a good exercise to do whenever you feel unwell or rundown. It can also be used to raise your spirits if you are feeling downcast or despondent.

5. Hold the picture in your mind for as long as possible. When you feel ready, open your eyes, stretch, and sense the vitality and power within you.

An actor friend of mine uses this exercise for confidence. Although he is an experienced actor, he still suffers from nerves before each performance. After doing this exercise he feels so full of power and energy that all the tension and stress is eliminated and he can walk onto the stage feeling confident and strong.

You can use this exercise to talk to your three selves, also. If you are feeling unwell, speak to your Low Self. The replies will come as thoughts in your mind. Your Low Self looks after your physical body and will enable you to talk directly to any part of your body that is not operating as well as it should be. Once you have done that, you should talk to your High Self and ask for healing and guidance. Obviously, if the problem is serious, you should also consult your health professional and follow his or her advice.

Keep on top of your thinking when doing any form of self-healing. You might use affirmations such as, "My shoulder is healing rapidly. I am returning to vibrant health." In addition, perform the Kahuna rite at least once a day until your health is perfect again.

Healing Others with Kahuna Power

You can use the Eight Steps to a Miracle exercise for self-healing, but this can not be used if you are sending healing energy to someone else. Fortunately, there are two Kahuna methods for healing others: one if the person is with you, and the second for absent healing.

Method One

1. Sit down with the person who you are going to send healing energy to. Ask him or her to relax, while you do the first part of the process. Make sure that you allow enough time at this stage to relax your mind and body.

2. When you feel ready, stand with your feet about eighteen inches apart and take four deep breaths in the usual way.

Imagine that you are filling your Low Self with healing mana.

3. Again, when you feel ready, allow this mana to shoot upwards to your High Self. Picture it as a cloud of white energy above your head.

4. Inside this cloud visualize the person you are intending to heal, but picture him or her fully restored to health.

5. Say to your High Self: "I want healing energy for (person's name). Please restore him/her to vibrant health and vitality. I ask this of you Great Father (or whatever name you choose to call your High Self)."

6. Wait until you feel a response in your body. This is likely to be a feeling that it is time to proceed with the ritual. However, you may experience it in a variety of ways. You may feel a sense of warmth, coolness, or a physical sensation on your arms or shoulders.

7. Hold your palms about twelve inches apart and take four more deep breaths. You are likely to feel a sense of warmth in the palms of each hand.

8. If the person is ill in a specific part of the body, hold your hands a few inches away from each side of this area, with the palms of your hands facing each other. Hold this position for sixty seconds.

9. Place your hands on the part of the body that needs healing. Alternatively, rest the palms of your hands on the person's shoulders. Again, hold this position for sixty seconds. The laying on of hands is a particularly good way of transferring mana energy from one person to another. If the person is ill, but there is no specific area to be healed, you can send healing energy to every part of the person's body by the laying on of hands.

10. After spending a minute on the specific area that needs healing, ask the person to stand up. Stand on one side of the person, and, with your palms next to each other, slowly bring them from the top of the person's head down to the feet. The palms of your hand should be about three inches away from the person's body at all times.

11. After doing this, turn away from the person and shake both hands vigorously. This is to release the negativity that your hands will have picked up from the patient. Take four more deep breaths to fill yourself again with mana, and repeat this on the other side of the person's body.

12. Repeat this stage with the person's front and back, remembering to shake your hands vigorously each time.

13. Finally, ask the person to take four slow, deep breaths. Do this exercise with him or her. This restores your mana, and also provides additional mana for your patient.

14. Repeat as often as possible, ideally on a daily basis, until the person is restored to full health.

Method Two (Absent Healing)

Whenever possible, ask the person you are planning to send healing to for permission first. Everybody follows their own path through life, and some will not appreciate anyone sending healing to them. This may sound strange, but some people have a vested interest in being sick. It may bring them sympathy or the attention that they subconsciously felt was lacking when they were well. They may even be ideologically opposed to any form of alternative healing. You must respect their wishes. If they don't want healing, ask if you can pray for them. I have yet to have someone refuse to let me do this.

Obviously, if someone is unconscious, or you are unable to contact them for some reason, you can send mana to his or her High Self. Ask that it be used for that person's best possible interest.

1. Relax in a comfortable chair and think about the person who requires your healing energies.

2. When you feel ready, stand up and fill your Low Self with mana.

3. Send this to your High Self and visualize it as a cloud of energy over your head. Mentally place the person you are sending healing to inside this cloud. However, the picture you visualize must show him or her enjoying radiant health.

4. Hold this picture in your mind for as long as you can, and then ask your High Self to send this mana to the High Self of the person you are wanting to help. You might say: "Great Father, would you please send this gift of healing mana to my friend, (person's name). My friend wants good health again, and I am grateful for your help. Thank you."

5. Take four more deep breaths, to fill your body with mana. Close your eyes, and visualize this mana leaving your body from the area of your heart, and racing toward your friend.

6. Give thanks to each of your three selves, and carry on with your day, confident that both the mana you have sent, and the help you have gained from your High Self, will benefit your ill friend. You will also, as a by-product, have established or strengthened the aka attachment between you and the person requiring healing.

The methods of the Kahunas almost disappeared from history, and it is fortunate that dedicated people, such as Dr. William Tufts Brigham and Max Freedom Long managed to record it before it vanished forever. The Ha Rite enabled the Kahunas to contact the god within and perform miracles. You can use the same methods to achieve miracles in your life.

Five

Miracles of Intuition

THE ANCIENT KAHUNAS used their High Self to gain access to their intuition. Now that you have practiced some of their techniques, you can start performing miracles of intuition.

Intuition is the art of gaining knowledge without the use of any of the five normal senses of sight, hearing, smell, touch, and taste. It is a sixth sense, that everyone possesses. Have you ever experienced a hunch or gut feeling about something? That is your intuition in action. A thought or feeling suddenly came into your mind, bypassing the normal reasoning processes.

Surveys of top business executives show that many of their decisions are made by acting on their hunches. They use reason and logic most of the time, of course, but when they get a sudden feeling about something, they act on it. A friend of mine has started and operated more than a dozen businesses in the time that I have known him. He has an incredible knack of knowing what type of business is likely to be successful at any given time. Consequently, he is normally a few steps ahead of everyone else with each new venture. He is equally as good at knowing when to sell, and usually sells out just a few months after the demand for whatever it is he is offering has reached its peak.

Other business owners are always asking him for his "secrets." They are seldom satisfied when he tells them that he simply follows his feelings. He is one person who is using his intuition to achieve astonishing success. His rags to riches story is a miracle. I find it fascinating that he uses his intuition so incredibly well in business, but fails to use it in other areas of his life. People who attain success in every area of life are rare, but it is something we should all aspire to achieve. Then our whole lives become a miracle to behold.

Extrasensory perception can be divided into a number of areas: telepathy, clairvoyance, precognition and psychokinesis. Telepathy is the ability to send and receive thoughts. It is frequently known as mind to mind communication. Clairvoyance does not need the presence of another mind. It is the ability to psychically perceive information that is not consciously known. When someone uses clairvoyance, he or she "knows" the answer. Precognition, or premonition, is the art of knowing future events. Psychokinesis is slightly different to the other three, and is the ability to mentally influence an object or event. Gamblers attempt this whenever they try to mentally influence the throw of dice.

It is important to remember that our intuition is working all the time. We can use it consciously, if we choose, but it also works subconsciously throughout our lives to help and protect us. Often, subconscious intuitions come to us in the form of dreams, or when we are doing something fairly mundane, such as washing the dishes.

For the purposes of miracles, the two most useful forms of extra sensory perception are clairvoyance and precognition.

Clairvoyance

Clairvoyance is the ability to gain impressions of something without using the usual five senses. The five senses of seeing, hearing, touching, tasting and smelling, are considerably enhanced when a sixth sense—knowing—is added. When you consciously dull the five senses, you allow your sixth sense to come into its own. When you make use of this knowingness, you are channeling information from the universal mind, into your subconscious mind, and then into your conscious awareness.

You may have done this at special moments in the past when you were suddenly in tune with the universe. You may have gained sudden information about something or someone that you could not have learned in any other way. Fortunately, you do not need to wait for those special moments to reoccur. Clairvoyance is a natural ability that everyone can develop.

The first step is to relax. This is essential for any psychic activity. It is difficult to receive any clairvoyant impressions when you are tense or stressed. Choose a time and place where you are unlikely to be disturbed. Sit down in a comfortable chair, close your eyes, take a few deep breaths and concentrate on relaxing all of the muscles of your body.

When you feel completely relaxed physically, still your mind as well. This is not easy to do, as our minds are busy all the time. As much as possible, eliminate all conscious thought, so that anything that comes into your mind will arrive there clairvoyantly.

You may experience clairvoyant impressions as thoughts, feelings, tastes, smells, sounds, or pictures. Sometimes a number of these may be used at the same time to create a clear impression. Try not to evaluate anything that comes to you until afterwards, as clairvoyant impressions are fragile and easily lost when the conscious mind becomes involved.

Strictly speaking, clairvoyance means to "see" something that is not known. Hearing things, for instance, is properly named clairaudience, and sensing something is known as clairsentience. However, for the sake of convenience, information that comes through by paranormal means is said to have arrived clairvoyantly.

Chester Carlson, the inventor of the Xerox copying machine credited clairaudience for his success. One night, while working in his home laboratory, a voice taught him how to make carbon jump onto a charged drum, and then imprint copies onto sheets of paper. To show his gratitude to the universe for providing him with this information, Carlson donated millions of dollars toward psychic research.[1]

A well-authenticated instance of clairvoyance occurred in 1756 when Emmanuel Swedenborg (1688–1772) received clairvoyant impressions of a fire that was raging in Stockholm, three hundred miles away. Swedenborg went into a trance while at a reception in Gothenberg, and told the people there about the progress of the fire as it was raging. When a courier arrived the next day, bringing news of the fire, it was found that Swedenborg's clairvoyancy had been correct in every detail.

In his book *Powers That Be*, Beverley Nichols recounted a fully documented instance of spontaneous clairvoyancy. He was doing a live radio report on the British royal family for the Canadian Broadcasting Company. He decided to finish his report with a description of the Queen driving down the Mall in a coach. As he spoke about this, he experienced the sudden onset of a headache, and a clear picture came into his mind of President Kennedy driving in an open car, with motorcycle escort. The producer of the program was delighted, as it enabled Beverley Nichols to compare the enormous security required for the president of the United States with the laid-back approach necessary for the royal family. Once the report was over, the broadcast team went for a drink. A man approached them on the street and told them that President Kennedy had been assassinated several minutes earlier, at the exact moment that Nichols received his unexpected headache.[2] The only discrepancy was that Beverley Nichols had pictured President Kennedy in New York, rather than Dallas.

A good way to develop your clairvoyancy skills is to hold an object and see what impressions come to you. This is known as psychometry. Sit down quietly, relax, hold or fondle the item, and see what happens. It might take several minutes for any impression to come through the first time you try this. However, with practice, impressions will come into your mind almost as soon as you move into a clairvoyant state of mind. Some psychometrists are able to divine the entire history of an object when they hold or touch it.

Here is what Mrs. Anna Denton, a nineteenth-century psychometrist, said while holding a fragment of a mastodon tooth:

> My impression is that it is a part of some monstrous animal, probably part of a tooth. I feel like a perfect monster, with heavy legs, unwieldy head, and a very large body. I go down to a shallow stream to drink. I can hardly speak, my jaws are so heavy. I feel like getting down on all fours. What a noise comes through the wood. I have an impulse to answer it. My ears are very large and leathery, and I can almost fancy they flap my face as I move my head. There are some older ones than I. It seems, too, so out of keeping to be talking with these heavy jaws. They are dark brown, as if they had been completely tanned. There is one old fellow, with large tusks, that looks very tough. I see several young ones; in fact, there is a whole herd.[3]

As you can see, the amount of information that can be received this way is incredible. Mrs. Denton appeared to actually become a mastodon for the length of time that she was holding the fragment of tooth.

Charles Inman psychometrized letters to gain insights about the writers of them. He was a protégé of Dr. Joseph Rodes Buchanan (1814–1899), a lifelong student of psychometry and author of a lengthy book on the subject called *Manual of Psychometry* (1889).

Dr. Buchanan noticed how accurate Charles Inman was at psychometrizing people by running his hands over their heads, and decided to see if he could psychometrize letters in the same way. He chose four letters from his files, each written by a person of strong character. When he picked them up, Charles Inman was able to talk about the letter-writers as if he had known them all his life. Two of the letters had been written by two people who had formerly been friends, but were now enemies. Inman picked this up instantly, and found the emotions induced to be so strong that he had to put the letters down. Dr. Buchanan asked him which one of the two would win in a conflict. Inman immediately held up a letter and said: "This one would crush the other." He was correct again, as this person had been responsible for causing the other to lose his position.4

Be patient. Experiment regularly, and keep notes of your progress. Clairvoyancy is a useful skill that can enhance your life in many ways.

How to Predict Your Own Future

What could be more miraculous than to be able to part the veil and gain glimpses of the future? Prophecy, divination, precognition, premonition, augury, foresight, second sight, and fortunetelling are all terms used to describe the ability to foretell future events. Throughout history, certain gifted people have been able to do exactly that. Yet parapsychological research today seems to indicate that everyone has this gift, but it needs nurturing and encouragement to develop.

Predictions have always been popular. The Oracle of Apollo, at Delphi, was just one of a number of oracle temples that were popular during the Greek civilization. King Croesus of Lydia tested many oracles, and was impressed when the Delphic oracle correctly announced that Croesus was cooking a lamb and a tortoise in a brazen pot. This was a most unusual thing for a king to be doing. Encouraged by this, Croesus asked about a military campaign he was contemplating. The oracle replied that it would result in the destruction of a great army. Assuming that this meant his enemy, Croesus went ahead, but the great army that was destroyed was his own.

One of the greatest military encounters in ancient history, the Battle of Salamis, was the direct result of a prophecy from the Delphic oracle. Around 480 BCE, the Persians, under the leadership of Xerxes, decided to attack Athens. He built 1,400 huge ships to carry his army across the Aegean Sea. As soon as the Athenians heard about this threat, they consulted the oracle. The prognosis was not good. The oracle advised everyone to leave Athens and to put their faith into walls of wood. Half the population refused to leave, while the others went to Piraeus and built three hundred wooden ships. The Persians duly sacked Athens, and then proceeded to attack the Greek ships. The Greeks lured the Persians into the Straits of Salamis, where the smaller Greek boats were able to ram and sink the clumsy Persian ships. The remaining Persian ships fled for home, leaving their soldiers behind. Most of them died, trying to return home by crossing the mountains in the middle of winter. The Parthenon, the greatest

architectural wonder of the ancient world, was later built to com-
memorate this victory.

Eighteen of the thirty-nine books of the Old Testament start
with the words "The Book of the Prophet." Most people have
heard how Joseph interpreted the precognitive dreams of the
Pharaoh: "Behold, there come seven years of great plenty throughout all the land of Egypt: And there shall arise after them seven
years of famine" (Genesis 41: 29–30). Joseph, the earthly father of
Jesus, had a predictive dream that saved the life of the young child:
"The angel of the Lord appeareth to Joseph in a dream, saying,
Arise, and take the young child and his mother, and flee into Egypt,
and be thou there until I bring thee word: for Herod will seek the
young child to destroy him" (Matthew 2:13).

At the Last Supper, Jesus made a prediction when he said, "One
of you which eateth with me shall betray me" (Mark 14:17). He
made another when he told Peter, "Before the cock crow twice,
thou shalt deny me thrice" (Mark 14:30). Both of these predictions
came true.

Predictions still play an important role in life today. Weather
forecasters tell us what they think the weather will be like on a
certain day. Economic forecasters make predictions about the
economy. Gamblers make predictions on the outcome of horse
races. Behavioral psychologists can predict with uncanny accuracy how a certain person will behave in a given set of circumstances. Statisticians can predict the numbers of births, deaths,
murders, and suicides in a given period with uncanny accuracy.
All of these people are making predictions based on the information they already have.

However, some people seem to be able to transcend time and gain knowledge of future events without any advance information. These most commonly occur in dreams, or in that borderland state between being asleep and awake. Other people use devices of various sorts, such as the I Ching, Tarot cards, or crystal balls, to part the veil of the future.

An interesting example of this is the divining basket used by Bantu tribes in Africa. The divining basket is a woven basket, with a lid, containing some forty to eighty fetish-like objects. Each of these objects symbolizes something, or a certain aspect of village life. The diviner shakes the basket, and then makes a prediction based on the topmost object in the basket. Frequently, these prophecies prove to be correct.[5]

I have had a great deal of success with Sky Stones. The ancient Celts practiced a variety of forms of stone divination, as they believed that everything, even stones, possessed a spirit. Sky Stone divination is one of several forms of stone divination recorded in *The Books of Ffrryllt*, one of the ancient texts of Wales. Sky Stones are limited to "yes" and "no" answers, but are astonishingly accurate. You will need three stones, about an inch in diameter: one each of gold, silver and black. I use gold pyrite or tiger eye for the gold one, hematite for the silver, and obsidian for the black one. These colors symbolize the three Druidic thresholds of dawn (gold), dusk (silver), and midnight (black).

To use the stones, hold them together in one hand while you think of your question. Gently toss them onto a flat surface, and see which stone is closest to the black one. If the gold stone is nearer than the silver one, the answer is positive. If the silver one is closer, the answer is negative. If they are both exactly the same distance away from the black stone, the stones need to be tossed again. If you experiment with these, accept the answer that the stones give you. Do not keep tossing the stones in the hope of getting a different answer. The stones lose their effectiveness when doubted in this way.[6]

Parapsychologists have performed a variety of predictive experiments under laboratory conditions. The first experiments were conducted by Dr. J. B. Rhine in 1933. A subject who had shown ability at clairvoyance with ESP cards was asked to predict the order of the cards after they had been shuffled. The results were promising and encouraged the parapsychologists to continue with their tests.[7]

Dr. S. G. Soal, a mathematician at London University, tried to duplicate Dr. Rhine's experiments in England. His experiments with 162 people from 1934 to 1939 produced no evidence of ESP, and he began to question whether it existed at all.

Fortunately, a researcher named Whately Carington began conducting ESP experiments in Cambridge in 1939. One of these involved three hundred people who had to guess the random drawing he sent out each day. He discovered that he had little success on the evenings he sent out the drawing, but he found that many of his volunteers successfully guessed the drawing one or two days ahead of time, or one or two days later. This appeared to indicate both precognition and retrocognition. Carington suggested that Dr. Soal check his results again, to see if they showed this displacement effect. After much persuasion, Dr. Soal reluctantly agreed and found that two of his subjects were outstandingly good at consistently predicting the card that was one ahead of the one he had been projecting. Dr. Soal continued his experiments with these two subjects and received consistently good results. One of his subjects, Basil Shackleton guessed at the rate of one card every two and a half seconds, and constantly picked the card one ahead of the one being dealt. When Dr. Soal asked him to speed up to one card every 1.25 seconds, he began picking up the card two ahead. Statistically, the results obtained were billions to one against chance.[8] This appeared to be conclusive evidence of precognition.

Dr. Soal began by reporting that he had had no success, and even doubted Dr. Rhine's results. However, he had positive evidence of precognition all the time, but had not identified it. In 1955, an attempt was made by G. R. Price to show that Doctors Rhine and Soal had achieved their successful results by fraud. Sixteen years later, he backed down and retracted his charge.[9]

Helmut Schmidt, at one time the director of Dr. J. B. Rhine's parapsychology laboratory, devised an experiment that used the breakdown of strontium-90 atoms using electrons. The participants were asked to predict when the next electron in this random process would appear. In the first main experiment, three volunteers achieved results that were 4.4 percent higher than chance would indicate. The probability of this occurring by chance was less than one in five-hundred-million. In the second main experiment, the participants were given the choice of aiming for a larger or smaller number of hits. This was also successful. The people aiming for more hits were 7.1 percent ahead of the chance expectation, and the people aiming for fewer hits were 9.1 percent ahead of chance. The probability of this occurring by chance alone is less than one in ten billion.[10] However, the accuracy of these figures have been questioned by Dr. Schmidt's critics.[11]

Gerald Croiset, the Dutch psychic, was given a series of tests by Professor Willem Tenhaeff of the University of Utrecht. Dr. Tenhaeff would randomly choose a seat number at an unreserved public hall and ask Croiset to describe the person who would sit in that particular seat at a certain date in the future. Dr. Tenhaeff had total control of all the conditions, choosing both the hall that was to be used, the date, and the seat number. Croiset was not perfect, but he achieved many successes. On one occasion the hall selected was in Rotterdam, and the seat number was three. Croiset described a middle-aged woman from Milan, who lived over a butcher shop, and had a scar on her face from a recent automobile accident. Croiset was correct in every detail.[12]

Unfortunately, most chance predictions are of tragic events, usually concerning the death of the person, or someone close to him or her.

One intriguing example of this was related by the famous stage magician, Harry Kellar (1849–1922). In 1877, he was in Shanghai with two men who used the stage names of Ling Look and Yamadeva. Despite these different names, they were brothers. Shortly before leaving for Hong Kong, Yamadeva and Kellar visited a bowling alley. They watched a sea captain using a large, heavy ball, and Yamadeva decided to try one that was just as heavy. He picked it up and, with all the effort he could muster, threw it down the alley. He immediately grasped his side in agony, and was barely able to return to the ship. He went to bed and died shortly afterwards. An autopsy showed that he had ruptured an artery. The ship's captain did not want to take the body to Hong Kong, but Kellar and Ling Look managed to persuade him.

As the ship sailed down the Yang Tse Kiang River, Ling Look, not surprisingly, felt depressed. However, he suddenly cheered up when he heard the unusual whistle that he and his brother used to call each other. The whistle was repeated several times and everyone on board heard it. The captain, feeling that something was wrong, agreed to take the lid off the coffin, and confirmed that Yamadeva was definitely dead.

Ling Look began sobbing, and told Harry Kellar that he would not be alive by the time the ship reached Hong Kong, as his brother was calling him. When Ling Look reached Hong Kong, he immediately needed a liver operation, and died without regaining consciousness. Ling Look's prediction that his brother was calling him proved to be correct.[13]

This, of course, makes one wonder if Ling Look could have changed this destiny. In actuality, he probably wanted to be reunited with his brother, but what if he had wanted to live? There are many recorded instances which seem to indicate that he might have been able to change his fate.

A friend of Arthur W. Osborn, author of an excellent book on precognition, *The Future is Now*, did exactly that. He was a music teacher at an English public school. One day he was watching a pupil play the piano when the music appeared to vanish, to be replaced by a scene of a road he would be driving along later that afternoon. As he watched, a car came around a bend on the wrong side of the road, driving extremely fast. The scene rapidly faded, and he could see the music again. That afternoon, as he was driving along the same stretch of road, he remembered the vision, and stopped the car on the other side of the road. As he did this, a car came around the corner on the wrong side of the road, driving extremely fast, exactly as in his premonition.[14]

Another interesting example involved Sir Winston Churchill. During the air raids in London during the Second World War, Churchill regularly used to visit the civil defense forces to help boost morale. He always sat on the near side of the car. One night, his driver opened this door for him, but Churchill, after looking at the open door, walked around the car, opened the door on the other side, and got in. He had never done this before. Thirty minutes later, a bomb landed near the off-side of the car, and the force of the explosion raised that side of the car off the ground. The car almost somersaulted, but righted itself just in time. Churchill did not tell his wife of this incident, to avoid worrying her, but she heard about it from the driver. When she asked her husband why he walked around the car and got in on the off-side, he said he did not know. When she stared hard at him, he added: "Yes I do know. When I got to the near-side door held open for me, something in me said 'Stop, go round to the other side and get in there,' and that is what I did."[15]

If precognition can occur in personal cases, such as these, surely it must be possible for people to predict major disasters. William Lilly (1602–1681) was a well-known astrologer who, in 1648, published his predictions of the Great Plague and the Great Fire of London in his book *Astrological Predictions*. "In the year 1665," he wrote, "the Aphelium of Mars, who is the general signification of England, will be in Virgo, which is surely the ascendant of the English monarchy, but Aries of the Kingdom. When the absis therefore of Mars, shall appear in Virgo, who shall expect less than a strange catastrophe of human affairs in the common wealth, monarchy and Kingdom of England . . . it will be ominous to London, unto her merchants at sea, to her traffique on land, to her poor, to all sorts of people, inhabiting in her or to her liberties, by reason of sundry fires and a consuming plague."[16] William Lilly made other predictions about the plague and fire in his book *Monarchy and No Monarchy*, published in 1651. Because his predictions proved so accurate in every detail, William Lilly was summoned before a commission set up to investigate the disasters on October 25, 1666. He reported that he was treated well by the commission who were satisfied that he had made his predictions based solely on his astrological calculations.

In 1912, a marine engineer named Colin Macdonald had a strong premonition that some disaster would happen to the Titanic and turned down three increasingly tempting offers to sign on as second engineer. The man who took his place was drowned.

W. T. Stead, the famous newspaper editor, was not as fortunate. Two fortunetellers had told him that he would drown on a ship sailing to America. Despite his interest in psychic matters, W. T. Stead booked a berth on the Titanic and died, exactly as the fortunetellers had predicted.[17]

In 1956, Jeane Dixon was interviewed by Jack Anderson of *Parade* magazine. In his article in the May 13 issue of the magazine, he wrote: "As for the 1960 election, Mrs. Dixon thinks it will be won by a Democrat. But he will be assassinated in office." This prediction came tragically true on November 22, 1963 when President Kennedy was shot in Dallas. In fact, Jeane Dixon had had a number of premonitions concerning the death of the president, starting in 1952. On the day President Kennedy was shot, Jeane Dixon had a vision of the White House shrouded in black. At breakfast that day, she said, "This is the day—this is the day; it has to happen."[18] In fact, Jeane Dixon had previously foretold the death of another president. In November 1944, President Roosevelt invited her to the White House and asked her how much time he had left to live. She told him that it would be six months, or less. He died five months later.[19]

A nine-year-old girl in Wales had a disturbing premonition. She told her mother, "I'm not afraid to die, Mummy, because I shall be with Jesus."

"Why do you talk like that?" her mother asked.

"Because everything is so black all around me," she said. The next morning, October 21, 1966, a huge slag tip slid down a mountainside, and killed 128 children at the Aberfan school. The girl was buried in the avalanche.[20] After the Aberfan mine disaster, the *London Evening Standard* asked their readers if they had received any premonitions about it. Seventy-six people wrote in, claiming to have had premonitions beforehand. Twenty-four of these people had told their premonitions to others before the accident. Many mentioned a black, slimy substance, and one man gave the name "Aberfan."[21]

By far the most commonly received premonitions are those of disasters. In many cases, it seems that foreknowledge of these can avert the tragedy. Dr. Louisa E. Rhine recorded the case of a mother who dreamed that in two hours a violent storm would cause a heavy chandelier to break loose from the ceiling and land on her baby's head. In her dream, she saw that her baby had died. She woke her husband and told him about it. He said it was a silly dream and she should forget about it. As the weather outside was calm, the woman thought she was being ridiculous, but, all the same, she brought the baby back to bed with her. Two hours later, exactly at the time specified in the dream, the chandelier fell where the baby's head would have been. Acting on this premonition saved the baby's life.[22]

It even appears that people can intuitively avoid disasters without knowing that they are doing so. An American researcher, William E. Cox, investigated twenty-eight serious railroad accidents. He discovered that the number of passengers traveling by train on the days of the accidents was significantly lower than on the same day in previous weeks. People either slept in, decided not to go work that day, felt ill on the days the accidents occurred, or for some other reason decided not to travel that particular day.[23]

This hypothesis appears to explain the experience of Sir Alec Guinness, the famous actor. While appearing in a play in London, he attended early mass every Sunday morning before returning to his home in the country on the 9:50 A.M. train. He was naturally an early riser, but to ensure that he got to mass, he always set two alarm clocks. On one occasion he slept through both alarm clocks, and then misread the time when he awoke. It was not until he was in church that he realized he was attending the 9:00 a.m. service, and would miss his normal train home. When he arrived at the station to book a later train, he learned that the train he would have been on had derailed. Later, he discovered that the front coach, where he always sat, had landed on its side, and several of the occupants had to be taken to the hospital.[24]

This section would not be complete without mentioning the man who was possibly the greatest seer of all time, Michel de Nostredame, better known as Nostradamus (1503–1566). Many people have told me that his predictions are worded in such a way that they could mean anything. In fact, this was essential. Predicting future events was a dangerous occupation and Nostradamus was forced to write them in such a way that only the knowledgeable few would understand them. One of his minor successes has always amused me. At one time he stayed at a castle in Lorraine owned by Seigneur de Florinville, a man who did not believe that anyone could predict the future. To prove this, he took Nostradamus to see two piglets, one white and the other black, and asked him to predict their future. "You will eat the black one, and a wolf will eat the white one," Nostradamus said. The Seigneur was determined to prove Nostradamus wrong. He told his cook to kill the white piglet and serve it for dinner that night. The pig was killed and cooked, and left on a table to be dressed. While the cook was out of the room, a wolf-cub who some of the servants had been trying to tame, got into the kitchen and ate it. Consequently, the cook killed the black piglet and served it for dinner instead. While they were enjoying the meal, the Seigneur took great pleasure in telling Nostradamus that his prediction was wrong, and that they were eating the white pig. Nostradamus insisted they were eating the black pig. The cook was called in, and agreed that Nostradamus was, in fact, correct.[25] Nostradamus' prophecies are still worthy of careful study today. One hundred years before William Lilly, he predicted the Great Plague and the Fire of London, and four hundred years before Jeane Dixon he predicted the death of President Kennedy.[26]

Developing Your Own Precognitive Skills

As you have seen, premonitions can occur to anyone. You do not have to be Nostradamus or Joan of Arc to receive precognitive messages. In fact, during your life, you have probably received hundreds, if not thousands, of premonitions in your dreams. Most of these would have been minor predictions, but if you had written them down at the time, you would have been able to verify them when they occurred.

Abraham Lincoln's premonitory dream of his death is well known. He told his wife and a friend, Ward H. Lamon, about a strange dream he had had in which he heard sounds of mourning. In his dream, Lincoln went from room to room in the White House, until he stepped in to the East Room. Here "there was a sickening surprise. Before me was a catafalque on which rested a corpse wrapped in funeral vestments. Around it were stationed soldiers who were acting as guards, and there was a throng of people, some gazing mournfully at the corpse."[27] The face of the corpse was covered, and Lincoln asked who it was. He was told that the president had been killed by an assassin. One week later, on April 14, 1865, the dream came true when Abraham Lincoln was assassinated by John Wilkes Booth.

Samuel Clemens, later to become world famous as the author Mark Twain, experienced a dream in which his brother, Henry, who worked on the same Mississippi River steamboat as he did, died. In his dream, Henry was lying in a metal casket. A spray of white flowers, with a red rose in the center, was lying on his chest. Clemens told his sister of the dream when he awoke, but then discarded it as a strange, but silly, dream. When he returned to his boat, he found that he had been transferred to another steamship. He said goodbye to Henry, and the two brothers agreed to meet in Memphis. Henry's boat, the Pennsylvania, left a day ahead of the A. T. Lacey, the boat that Clemens had been transferred to. When they reached Memphis they learned that the Pennsylvania had burst into flame just as it approached Memphis. Clemens tracked down his badly wounded brother in a temporary hospital. He stayed by Henry's bedside for four days and nights, until Henry died. When he arrived at the funeral home, he found it full of the bodies of the other victims. Henry was the only one in a metal casket. This, Clemens was told, was a gift from the ladies of Memphis who had been taken with Henry's youth and good looks. As Clemens looked down at his brother, a lady came up to the casket and placed a bouquet of white flowers, with a single red rose in the center, on his chest.

Most premonitions that come in the form of dreams are connected to a disaster of some sort. However, good news can also come in the form of a dream. The late Sir Ernest Wallis Budge (1857–1934) was a world authority on ancient languages and spent thirty years as the Keeper of the Department of Egyptian Antiquities at the British Museum. Many of his books are still in print today. He credited a fortunate dream as the pivotal point of his whole life. While studying at Cambridge University, Budge entered an Oriental languages competition. The prize was a fellowship that would enable him to continue with his studies. Budge was desperate to win the competition, and studied so hard that on the night before the competition, he went to bed mentally and physically exhausted. He dreamed that he was sitting the examination in a shed, rather than a lecture room. A tutor brought in the test questions, which were written on long strips of green paper that he produced from an envelope in his pocket. Some of them contained texts that needed to be translated. Budge could see that the questions themselves were easy for him to answer, but the texts were written in the little-known Akkadian language. In his dream, Budge panicked, thinking he would not be able to translate the text. This woke him up. He fell back to sleep, and dreamed the same dream again. At the end of the dream, he woke up, fell back to sleep, and dreamed the same dream again. After the third dream, Budge checked his bedside clock and found it was just after 2 A.M. He thought about the dream and remembered that the texts that needed to be translated were in a book he had in his study. He got out of bed, and studied the texts until it was time to leave for the examination.

Budge arrived early, but the examination room was full. He was taken to a small room that looked exactly like a shed. It contained one chair and a table, exactly the same as the ones he had seen in his dream. The tutor came in, took four slips of green paper out of an envelope that he had in his pocket, and gave them to Budge. The questions and the texts to be translated were exactly the same as the ones he had seen in his dream. Because he had studied the texts to be translated for several hours before the examination, Budge won the competition easily, and was able to embark on the career he had spent so many years striving for.[28]

The dreams of Abraham Lincoln and Mark Twain are well known, and are remembered, not only because they were famous, but because they were both told to others before the tragedy. E. A. Wallis Budge did not tell others about his dream until well after the event. However, precognitive dreams are not the preserve of the famous. It appears that everyone has them.

In 1927, J. W. Dunne wrote a book called *An Experiment With Time*, which described a number of his own precognitive dreams.[29] He felt that life was similar to film going through a projector. He hypothesized that in our dreams we can move forward to see what is on the roll of film before it is projected. The most exciting aspect of this book for his readers was that Dunne's dreams contained normal, everyday predictions. Most of Dunne's dreams contained predictions of what would happen to him the following day. They included amazingly accurate impressions of what was going to occur, but at the same time, they would be full of errors and distortions. Dunne believed that everyone has precognitive dreams, but we forget them as soon as we wake up. His advice was to keep a pad and pen beside the bed, and write down everything you can remember as soon as you wake up.

This advice is still as good as it was in 1927, although nowadays, many people prefer to record their dreams on to a cassette recorder. Everyone dreams, but they usually disappear from our memories as soon as we get up. If you find it hard to recall your dreams, lie still in bed for a few minutes, and see what comes into your mind. You might find it best to do experiments of this sort in the weekend, or at any other time when you do not have to leap out of bed as soon as you wake up. Once you get into the habit of writing down your dreams, you will quickly discover how many of them predict aspects of your future. You will also find out how long they take, on average, to be fulfilled. Warning dreams, for instance, may appear to deal with the immediate future, but actually relate to something months ahead. Keeping records of your dreams will enable you to time your precognitive dreams with much greater accuracy than would otherwise be the case.

Retrocognition

Retrocognition is the ability to divine past events that are not in your memory. The most extraordinary account of retrocognition I have come across involved two Oxford dons, Annie Moberly and Eleanor Jourdain. When they visited Versailles they were suddenly transported back into the eighteenth century, and experienced the sights, sounds, and people that were there at the time of Marie Antoinette and King Louis XVI. The people they met—gardeners, villagers, and noblemen and women—wore the correct clothes for the era, and spoke in an old-fashioned, archaic French. They even saw buildings that existed at the time, but had been demolished since. Both women reported that they had felt nervous and anxious while undergoing this strange experience. They published their account of what happened in *An Adventure in 1911*, using the pseudonyms of Miss Morison and Miss Lamont. Many people were skeptical of their story, but further details about Versailles in 1770 have come to light since they wrote their book, and so far their experiences have proved to be correct in every detail.[30]

You are using retrocognition all the time, but probably think it is simply a function of your memory. Think of an occasion when you accidentally bumped into someone you had not seen for a long time. You can not think of his name, so you mentally think back to where you saw him last. It might have been in a restaurant or his place of work, perhaps. As you do this, various links come into your mind to help you remember the person's name. Just one link is required, but you may have to picture several of them before the name suddenly arrives in your mind.

You are using your imagination to mentally relive scenes from your past. Not all of these may have happened. You may be picturing this person in a familiar setting in an attempt to divine his name. Consequently, you are creating a psychic recall of the past, and this is known as retrocognition.

I had an example of this recently. I was giving a talk at a Rotary Club, and happened to see someone in the audience who I knew. I had not seen him for many years, and had no idea that he belonged to this particular club. As I continued with the talk, I kept trying to think of his name. I started off in the wrong direction by trying to see him at work. This produced no links. I then wondered if he had attended one of my psychic development classes. Again, nothing came to mind. I wondered if he had been a hypnotherapy client of mine, but found no links there. I thought of a few other possibilities, and then wondered if I had met him at a social occasion. Instantly, the link came to me. About twenty years earlier, our then neighbor had had a party, and I had met this man there. As soon as I recalled that, his name came back to me, and I was able to greet him by name once I had finished the talk.

You can use the same technique to look into the future. Precognition, as you know, is a psychic vision of the future. Instead of looking back and recalling forgotten facts, you look ahead, replacing recall with vision. You can do this for both small and large matters. Suppose you are planning a dinner party, and are not sure if a certain couple will get on with the other dinner guests. Sit down comfortably, close your eyes, and project yourself forward to the evening of the proposed party. See yourself sitting at the dining-room table with your guests, and visualize what is going on. You are likely to experience snippets of conversation, and will definitely experience the mood and feelings of the evening. As a result of this exercise, you will be able to make an informed decision on whether or not to invite this couple.

Naturally, with something minor, such as a dinner party, the impressions may not be strong. However, if the issue is important, the impressions you receive will be powerful. You may have had a situation when you were warned about impending danger. Obviously, in this instance, the impression would be extremely strong.

About twenty years ago, I went for an evening walk around Suva, the capital of Fiji. I had visited the town many times before, and had always felt safe there. As I walked, a muscular Fijian came out of the darkness, and walked along with me. He was a good conversationalist, and it took me a while to realize that he was leading me into a poorer part of town that I had not been in before. I had a sudden feeling of foreboding. I said good night to the man, and quickly retraced my steps. When I returned to my hotel, I wondered if I had been over cautious. However, the next day I heard that another tourist had been beaten and robbed just an hour after my hasty retreat. In this instance, I did not wait to receive a mental picture of what might happen. The feeling of imminent danger was so strong that I immediately acted upon it.

Developing Your Precognition Skills

This is a pleasant exercise that you can do at any time. As you know, many people experience predictive dreams. This is because the body is relaxed, the conscious mind at rest, and the subconscious mind is able to receive messages from the universal mind. This exercise allows you to achieve this state while still awake.

Ensure that you will not be disturbed for at least thirty minutes. Sit down comfortably, close your eyes, and allow your mind to drift back until you recall an event from your past. It makes no difference when this event occurred. It might be yesterday, last week, or thirty years ago. Recall the event as clearly as you can. You will probably have to use your imagination to help you create some of the details, but try to picture the situation exactly as it was.

Once you have successfully pictured this scene in your mind, allow yourself to drift forward in time so you can envision a scene from your future. You might visualize something that will happen in the next day or two, or you might wish to see your future several years from now. It is better to start by looking at the next few days, as you will be able to confirm your accuracy almost immediately. As you gain confidence and experience, you will be able to picture scenes that are further into the future. Obviously, you will be using your imagination, but the scenes you see will be based on what you already know. This technique uses all the knowledge and experience you have gained in this lifetime, and projects it into the future. Naturally, practice is necessary to develop your ability to see into the future. Your success rate will increase as you gain confidence and skill.

Obviously, there will be occasions when you are not happy with what you see. Fortunately, you can change your future. Start with the present and see what changes you can make right away to alter the natural progression that would otherwise occur. It can be extremely useful to regularly look into your own future to ensure that you are attracting all the good things of life to you.

I had a striking example of this about thirty years ago. A young man came to me for a palm reading. On his life line I saw a number of small squares. The type of square indicated several periods of confinement. It was a strong indication that he would be spending much of his future life in prison. I told him what the squares meant, and suggested that he change his way of life. When he came back to me several months later for another reading, the squares had disappeared. This man had obviously thought about his life, changed his ways, and effectively changed his entire future life.[31]

This is one major benefit of looking into your own future. You will notice many aspects of your life changing once you start using your precognitive skills regularly. You will feel more in control and have a clear sense of where you are going. It is a miracle to be able to control and direct your life in this way. However, the real miracle is that more people are not using this natural ability to enhance the quality of their lives.

Six

The Miracle of Magic

WHEN YOU USE the methods of the Kahunas, and act on your intuition, you are using a form of magic. Magic is generally regarded as a sequence of actions that enables the person doing it to make use of the mystical powers of the universe to obtain whatever it is that is desired. It could be described as setting a goal, and then performing certain actions to symbolize its achievement. It is an act of creation that allows your dreams to come true. In that sense, it is a miracle.

Sacred objects, talismans, and spells may all be involved in the process of magic and, consequently, some people believe that magic is evil. Black magic can be used to harm others, but white magic is used only for good purposes. White magic is what we are concerned with here.

Magic has been defined in many different ways. The well-known twentieth century occultist and author, Aleister Crowley, defined magic as "the Science and Art of causing Change to occur in conformity with Will."[1] Florence Farr, an important figure in the Order of the Golden Dawn, wrote: "Magic consists of removing the limitations from what we think are the earthly and spiritual laws that bind or compel us. We can be anything because we are All."[2] You could say that magic consists of attracting to us whatever it is that we want. The ability to do that consistently is certainly miraculous, but it is well within the bounds of possibility for anyone who is prepared to work hard to attain it. Someone who is able to control his or her life, and direct it toward specific goals, is a magician.

Magic uses the deeper levels of the unconscious mind to effect changes in the material world. There is nothing strange, evil, demonic, or supernatural about it. The magician is someone who knows how to harness the laws of nature, and direct them through the power of his or her will. Everyone does this unconsciously from time to time. If you have set a goal and achieved it, you have successfully performed magic. When you decide to do this consciously, you are making the first steps toward becoming a magician.

Magic goes back into humanity's prehistory when people danced, chanted, and performed ceremonies in an attempt to influence nature. They conducted rituals to ward off thunder and lightning, ensure fertility, enable the huntsmen to catch their prey, and to appease the gods. In fact, as both magic and religion are concerned with the effects of outside forces on human beings, they have been inextricably connected from the very start.

The ancient Egyptians effectively combined religion and magic, using magic words, amulets, and talismans to help their followers make their way to the afterlife. There are many surviving Egyptian and Mesopotamian texts containing magical spells on a variety of subjects, ranging from ensuring a good harvest to invoking the spirits of the dead.

The Greek mystery cults included magic in their rituals, and surviving papyruses from the first four centuries CE contain detailed instructions on the purifications and preparations necessary to achieve good results.

The Romans were also vitally interested in magic, and began using it for personal purposes, such as ensuring victory in sports, business, and love.

Magic remained part of the popular culture, but almost disappeared from sight until the Middle Ages. In 1320 CE, a papal bull defined magic as a heresy. The church believed magic was concerned with making pacts with the devil and his demons. As a result of this, the Inquisition accused many people of participating in Black Masses and Witches' Sabbaths.

However, magic as part of the alchemical tradition quietly proceeded, and magicians, such as Cornelius Agrippa and John Dee, were able to follow their careers with only a moderate amount of interference from the church and state. The general public accepted magic and magicians, and consulted these special people whenever necessary. In 1552, Bishop Hugh Latimer (circa 1485–1555) wrote: "A great many of us, when we be in trouble, or sickness, or lose anything, we run hither and thither to witches, or sorcerers, whom we call wise men . . . seeking aid and comfort at their hands."3 Robert Burton, wrote in his classic book, *Anatomy of Melancholy*: "Sorcerers are too common; cunning men, wizards, and white witches, as they call them, in every village, which, if they be sought unto, will help almost all infirmities of body and mind."4

In the nineteenth century, popular attitudes about magic changed, and people considered it to be a superstitious practice performed by primitive people. In the last hundred years there has been a revival of interest in the subject, and today more people than ever before are studying and practicing magic.

Getting Started in Magic

Magic has the potential to change your life for the better. It means taking control of your own life, to achieve your specific goals. You can set your sights on almost anything, as long as it does not hurt, or impinge on the rights of others. Obviously, you need to be realistic. If you are forty-five years old, overweight, and cannot swim, it is most unlikely that you will ever represent your country at swimming. However, if you are a teenager, are physically fit, and are already a good swimmer, you could use magic to help you achieve your swimming goals.

Likewise, you can use magic to help you find love and romance. However, you must not use magic to impel a certain person to fall in love with you. That might satisfy your desires, but it might be the complete opposite of what the other person wants. Magic of that sort is black magic, and most people who dabble in it pay a heavy price for their folly. Dion Fortune (1891–1946), the famous occultist and author, wrote: "Any attempt to dominate others, or in any way manipulate their minds without their consent, is an unwarrantable intrusion upon their free will and a crime against the integrity of the soul."[5] Consequently, when using magic to attract love, you should send out a message to the universe that you are seeking a particular type of person. You can be as specific as you wish, but you can not specify a certain person. As well as being harmful, it is also limiting. By performing the magic ethically, you might attract to you someone much better than the person you currently desire.

Magic works by harnessing your conscious and unconscious minds. With magic, you create a desire, and then send it to your unconscious mind, which acts on it and makes it a reality. As you can see, the methods used by the Kahunas are a form of magic.

You might ask why the unconscious mind would act on any desire that is sent to it. You have tens of thousands of thoughts every day, most of which are ignored by the unconscious mind. With magic, you consciously send the desire to your unconscious mind with all the energy and power you can muster. This is created by the ritual performance of the magic. The reverse also occurs. When you are asleep, your conscious mind is at rest, but your unconscious mind remains active and sends thoughts and ideas to you in your dreams. The same thing occurs with meditation and self-hypnosis. Any hunch, feeling or sudden insight you gain while going about your everyday life is an example of information that has been sent to your conscious mind by your unconscious. It works ceaselessly for you all the time. Usually the transfer of information flows in one direction only, but with magic you can reverse the flow to achieve your goals and dreams.

Finding the Right Working Environment

You will need somewhere private in which to work your magic. The ideal situation would be a room dedicated to this purpose, but this is a luxury that few people have. Most people use a bedroom or living room. A table or bench can become a temporary altar, and sacred items, such as candles and pictures, can be displayed and used while working, and then put away afterwards. I enjoy working outdoors during the summer months, but obviously I also have a sacred space indoors that I use when it is windy, wet, or cold.

You will need a compass to determine the four cardinal directions. Before starting your magical work you can sprinkle a small amount of salt water in these directions to purify the space.

Whenever possible, have a shower or bath before commencing any magical work. You will also need comfortable, loose-fitting clothes. A robe made of natural fibers, that is used only for magical work, would be ideal. Many people like to work skyclad (naked). By taking off their clothes, they symbolically shed all the cares and stresses of everyday life.

Preparing to Start

You need to be relaxed to gain the full benefits of your magical work. I like to perform some simple stretching exercises before starting. I then sit down comfortably and take several slow, deep breaths. I inhale to a count of five, hold it for another five, and then exhale to the same count.

Finally, I close my eyes and consciously relax all the muscles of my body, starting with my feet, and then working my way through the body to the top of my head. After doing this, I mentally scan my body to make sure that I am completely relaxed. I focus on any areas of tension that are still left, until the tension has gone. When I feel completely loose and limp, like a rag doll, I open my eyes and am ready to start.

Starting the Magic

I prepare to start in the same way every time. Because of this, I find myself completely relaxed almost as soon as I start on the five deep breaths. Starting in the same way each time is familiar and comforting, and also helps me become mentally ready for whatever is to follow.

Once you are fully relaxed, you can take the ritual in any direction you want. If you have no specific goal in mind, you can use this time for meditation and contemplation. You are likely to gain many useful intuitive insights as a result of this. Alternatively, you might like to perform a guided visualization, perform an absent healing on someone, or perform a spell.

Meditation

The purpose of meditation is to quieten the mind and spirit, creating a state of serenity and detachment. Once you reach this state, you are ready to receive messages from your unconscious mind. It is not as easy as it sounds, and I have met many people who are convinced that they cannot meditate. This is not true. It is a skill that anyone can learn, but it takes practice.

Make yourself as comfortable as possible. Close your eyes and take several slow, deep breaths, holding each breath for a second or two before slowly exhaling. Breathe through your nose, and feel the breath entering and exiting through your nostrils.

You are likely to be distracted easily, particularly when you first start. Whenever you find that your thoughts have strayed away from the meditation, simply bring them back by focusing on your breathing. This is likely to happen frequently when you first start practicing meditation, but after a few weeks of daily practice you will find it a simple matter to slip directly into a meditative state.

If you are like most people, you will experience itches in different parts of your body. Ignore these, if you possibly can. If you desperately need to scratch the itch, do so, but then immediately return to your meditation. After a while, you may feel uncomfortable. Again, ignore this if possible, but change position if you absolutely have to.

You will find that regular meditation helps open the channels between your conscious and unconscious minds, and a variety of ideas and symbols will occur to you while you are in this state. Try not to evaluate these while you are meditating. Keep them in your mind to think about later.

I find it comparatively simple to enter into a meditative state while out walking. I am not sure if this is because I walk every day, and find it invigorating, refreshing and good for my body and soul, or if it is because I use the time spent walking to quietly think about the various things that are going on in my life. Focus on your breathing, and start walking with steady, deliberate strides. After a while, you will suddenly find yourself in the meditative state. The hardest part of the entire process is ignoring all the distractions that can prevent you from entering into the meditation.

Another personal favorite method that I use frequently is candle meditation. All you need is a single candle. I always have a variety of colors to choose from, and will occasionally deliberately choose a certain color. At other times, the candle seems to choose me, and I find myself lighting a candle of a particular color without consciously choosing it. If I am undecided about the choice of color, I select a white candle. White can be used at any time, for any purpose, in candle magic.

Place the candle in a holder on your altar, and light it. Sit down in a comfortable chair, several feet away. You should be able to gaze at the candle without raising or lowering your head. Take a few deep breaths, while gazing at the dancing flame, and allow your body to relax. Concentrate on the air entering and leaving your nostrils while continuing to stare at the flame. Close your eyes at any time, if they want to close. Gradually, you'll find yourself entering into an altered state in which ideas, perceptions, and intuitions will flow into your conscious mind.

When you feel ready to end the meditation, take three slow deep breaths, stretch, and think about what came to you while performing the meditation. When you feel ready, get up and snuff out the candle.

An alternative method of candle meditation is to sit in front of the flame for a few minutes, watching its changing shapes and colors. Close your eyes, and try to capture the image of the candle in your mind. Hold that image for as long as you can. When it fades, remain receptive for any insights that come to you.

The Amazing Pendulum

The humble pendulum is a useful tool that can be used in many different ways. At its most basic, it is a small weight attached to a piece of thread. My mother used to use her wedding ring, suspended on a piece of cotton, as a pendulum. I have a huge selection of pendulums, as my children regularly buy me small objects, attached to chains, for birthday and Christmas presents. I also have several commercially made pendulums that I have bought at New Age stores. Experiment with different types of pendulum. A good pendulum should be attractive to look at, easy to use, and have a weight of about three ounces.

Hold the thread of your pendulum between the thumb and first finger of your right hand. Use your left hand if you are left-handed. Rest your elbow on a table, and hold your hand so that the weight of the pendulum is swinging freely a few inches above the surface of the table.

Stop the movements of the pendulum with your free hand. Ask the pendulum which movement indicates "yes." The pendulum will make one of four movements. It might swing from side to side, or forward and backward. Alternatively, it might move in a circular motion, either clockwise or counter-clockwise. Be patient. If you have not used a pendulum before, it might take a minute or two to start moving. Once you have discovered which direction indicates a positive response, stop the movements and ask it which direction indicates "no." Once you have determined this, you can ask it to tell you which movements indicate "I don't know" and "I don't want to answer."

Once you have noted the meanings of each movement, you can practice. Ask the pendulum if you are male. If you are, the pendulum should give you a positive response. Ask it if you are, for example, thirty-two years old. The pendulum will move to agree or disagree.

Once you have received the correct answers to questions that you already know, you can proceed to the next stage and ask it questions that you are curious about. You might ask, "Am I doing enough exercise?" or "Should I take that trip to Disneyland?" The pendulum is easy to use, but it takes practice to become good at it. Experiment as much as possible, but do not concern yourself too much with the answers you receive until you feel totally comfortable with the pendulum.

You will find the pendulum an extremely useful tool in magic. If you desire a certain goal, for instance, you can ask your pendulum questions about it. You might ask if your spiritual growth would be enhanced by seeking a certain outcome. You might ask if a certain goal is realistic. Would it be beneficial for you to achieve it? Are you aiming high enough? Are there any unforeseen consequences? Would everyone benefit when you achieved this goal?

You can ask the pendulum anything at all. However, you must remain aware that you can, consciously or subconsciously, influence the movements of the pendulum. If you have a vested interest in the outcome, the pendulum will give you the answer that you desire, rather than the correct response. My mother always made a pendulum of her wedding ring when anyone in the family became pregnant, and asked it if the unborn child would be a boy or girl. Most of the time, she received the correct answer. However, on the occasions when she hoped the child would be, say, a girl, the pendulum would indicate that result, rather than whatever the true sex of the baby turned out to be.

The pendulum is a dowsing instrument. Most people consider dowsing to be a method of locating underground water, but it can, in fact, be used to locate almost anything. Jacques Aymar even used a forked stick, known as a dowsing rod, to track down a murderer. By the time he turned twenty-nine in 1692, Jacques Aymar had already made a name for himself locally as a dowser. However, when he successfully located one of the murderers of a wine merchant and his wife, his name was suddenly known throughout Europe.

The murder was a particularly nasty one, and the gendarmes found no clues in the cellar where the murders took place. Aymar had already located a number of criminals, and the king's procurator summoned him to see if he could dowse for clues.

Aymar used his forked dowsing stick to tell the gendarmes exactly where the murder had taken place. He then took to the streets, followed by a crowd of interested onlookers. His path took him directly to one of the city gates which had been closed for the night, so the search had to be postponed until the morning.

The following day, Aymr and three gendarmes followed a river until they found a small gardener's cottage. Aymar's dowsing rod reacted strongly to an empty wine bottle and three chairs. Aymar confidently told the gendarmes that they were in pursuit of three men who had stopped here long enough to drink a bottle of wine. This was confirmed by the gardener's two small children.

The chase continued until they reached a prison in the town of Beaucaire. Thirteen recently-arrested prisoners were lined up and Aymar's rod reacted to one of them, a hunchback who had been arrested only one hour earlier. Aymar told the gendarmes that this man had played a minor role in the murders.

The man denied any knowledge of the crime, but confessed when he was recognized by people returning from Lyon. He was a servant of the two men who had committed the murders, and had been employed to carry the silver and gold that was stolen from the victims.

The procurator was pleased with this success and commissioned him to find the real villains. Aymar and a group of archers followed the trail to the port of Toulon, where they were one day too late. The two murderers had left for Genoa in Italy the previous day.[6]

Guided Visualization (Pathworking)

Guided visualizations are an effective way of exploring your inner nature, and to see what your life will be like once you have achieved your goal. Every time we go into a daydream we are performing a type of visualization. However, most people exert no control over them, and our day dreams cover a huge range of topics that have nothing to do with what we really want out of life. A guided visualization is, as its name suggests, an extended, guided daydream in which we examine, feel, sense, and experience every aspect of the topic we are exploring.

There are two ways of performing them. The first is to have a clear idea in your mind as to where you want to go, and what you want to do, while conducting the visualization. The second method is to record on cassette tape everything you want to do in the session. You sit down, relax, and allow the voice on the tape to guide you through the experience.

There are advantages and disadvantages with both methods. A tape may rush you through areas that you want to explore in more depth. Because you are less consciously involved, you may fall asleep during the session. This is especially the case if you make the tape too long. I find twenty minutes to be about the right length of time from start to finish. (Most people speak about one-hundred-and-fifty words a minute, which means that if you are going to prepare a script, it should be no longer than three thousand words.) The main advantage of a prepared script is that you know in advance what will be covered. In fact, you can ensure that everything you want to do will be covered. You need have no concerns about forgetting anything that you want included. If you have not used guided visualizations before, it is better to start with a recorded script, and then experiment with more spontaneous visualizations once you are familiar with the process.

The disadvantage of not using a recorded script is that you can get side-tracked with random thoughts, and end up thinking about all sorts of things that are not related to your ultimate purpose. The main advantage I find with this method is that I do not have to prepare anything beforehand. I can decide to do the path-working whenever I wish, and then do it, without needing to find a cassette recorder and preparing a tape.

In practice, I use both methods. Sometimes I do this in bed at night. However, at least fifty percent of the time I fall asleep before commencing the visualization. Consequently, I usually set aside time during the day for this exercise. It is better not to lie down on a bed while doing a guided visualization, as the chances are high that you will drift off to sleep. A recliner-type chair makes a good alternative. You want to be comfortable, but not too comfortable.

Start by closing your eyes and taking three deep breaths. Consciously relax all the muscles of your body, starting with your feet and gradually working your way up to the top of your head. Once you feel completely relaxed, mentally scan your body to ensure that every part is totally relaxed. Focus on any areas that are not fully relaxed. When you are certain that you are completely relaxed you can start on the visualization.

In this state you can do anything. You can re-examine difficult times in your life to see if the events that occurred then are holding you back from achieving your goals. You can progress into the future, and see yourself enjoying a life full of joy and abundance. You can travel through time and space. You can meet your spirit guides and angel guardians. The visualization can be a total fantasy, if you wish. You might want to explore a favorite myth, and you can do this as an observer, or take on the role of the leading character. If you have a problem of any sort, you can use a guided visualization to spend time with famous people from the past, so that you can ask them for their insights and wisdom. You might visit these people one at a time, or possibly visualize a boardroom with all the people you want to talk to gathered around the table. There are no limits to what you can achieve.

When you are ready to return to full conscious awareness, simply take three deep breaths, and count slowly from one to five, opening your eyes when you reach the final number. Think about the visualization for a few minutes. You might want to make some notes, and think further about certain matters that came into your mind, before getting up and carrying on with your day.

Sample Script

One of my students was deeply in debt, and was concerned that he would go bankrupt. Josh, and his former partner, had operated a business together. When it failed, the relationship ended, and three years later he was still struggling to pay off business debts. He was also paying child support to his former wife, who was bringing up their two children. He was working as a warehouse manager, a job he hated, and one that paid only an average salary. He had just been told that the rent on his apartment was going up, and he was faced with either finding the extra money, or moving to a less desirable neighborhood where he could get cheaper accommodation. Josh needed a miracle.

After we had covered creative visualization in my psychic development class, Josh went home and prepared a script for himself. He played it every night for three weeks, not really believing that it would help. He did not notice any changes at all during the first week, but in the second week he found himself feeling more positive and optimistic than he had been in years. At the start of the third week, his work colleagues commented on the fact that he was whistling and making occasional jokes. During that week, he attended a Rotary club meeting. He had belonged to the club years before, but had dropped out when his business collapsed. Everyone was pleased to see him again, and one of the people there told him he was starting a new company and wanted good staff. Would Josh be interested? By the end of the week, Josh had been interviewed, and had accepted the task of managing the new corporation. His starting salary was exactly double what he was earning as a warehouse manager, and he had the option of buying stocks in the company. Josh declared it a miracle.

I have no idea what script Josh prepared for himself. However, it would have been something along the lines of this sample script.

"I am relaxing more and more with each easy breath I take. Every breath takes me deeper and deeper into pleasant relaxation. I enjoy taking slow deep breaths, as it makes me relax more and more. I am going to take three slow, deep breaths now, and I'll double my relaxation each time I exhale. I take the first deep breath now. Hold it. That's good, and now I exhale slowly, doubling the relaxation in my body. I take the second deep breath in.

It feels so good, and now I exhale slowly, feeling the relaxation spreading throughout my entire body. Third deep breath. Hold it, hold it, and exhale slowly. I feel so relaxed now, and each breath I take will send me even deeper into pleasant relaxation.

"My left foot is starting to relax even more. I can feel the pleasant relaxation spreading throughout my left foot, and now it is so relaxed. My right foot is also relaxing now. It feels wonderful to have both feet so totally relaxed. I'm now letting the pleasant relaxation drift up my left leg. It's a wonderful, soothing, restful feeling to know that I'm relaxing my entire body in this way. And now I'm allowing that relaxation to drift slowly up my right leg, relaxing my ankle, calf, and knees, and now the muscles in my thighs are relaxing. My legs feel totally loose, limp, and so relaxed.

"I'm allowing that pleasant feeling of relaxation to drift into my abdomen now. It's so peaceful and restful to relax like this, and I'm enjoying this wonderful feeling of relaxation as it drifts up into my chest and shoulders. All the stress and tension of everyday life is draining away from my shoulders, and I feel so loose and light, and so, so relaxed.

"The relaxation is drifting down my left arm now, all the way to the tips of my fingers. My left arm feels so totally loose and relaxed. The relaxation is moving into my right arm now, allowing the wonderful warm relaxation to drift all the way down to my fingertips.

"My arms, legs, and body are now loose, limp, and relaxed. And now, the muscles in my neck are relaxing too. I can feel the wonderful relaxation spreading up and into my face. The fine muscles around my eyes are relaxing now, and I sense the gentle relaxation reaching up to the very top of my scalp. My entire body is relaxed. I feel like a rag doll, so loose, so contented, so, so relaxed.

"I'm now scanning my entire body to make sure that every part of me is relaxed. I have no need for areas of tension. I'm comfortable, relaxed, and ready to proceed.

"What I need more than anything else is a miracle. I'm asking for a miracle. I've worked hard for many years, and I've got nothing to show for it. I'm in a worse financial state now than I was ten years ago. I'm a good worker, a hard worker. I'm loyal, kind, and caring. I believe that I deserve the very best that life has to offer. I know I've made many mistakes, but I've learned from them. I've let go of the bitterness and resentment I used to have. I've forgiven others, and I've forgiven myself. It's time for me to move on again.

"I'm working on self-development, and am gradually improving in all areas of my life, but right now I have huge financial pressures on me that are making it hard for me to focus on anything else. I need a miracle. I want an opportunity to double my net income. That will enable me to stay in my apartment, and continue to help support my children, while continuing to repay my debts. It will also give me extra money, to help me move ahead again. I need to double my net income.

"I'm prepared to do whatever is necessary to achieve this. All I want is an opportunity. After that, it's up to me. I know I can make it work, because I've worked hard all my life. I'm asking for an opportunity to double my net income. I need it, I desire it, and

I'm prepared to pay the price. I'm asking for this opportunity. Please bring it to me.

"In my mind's eye, I see myself sitting behind a desk in my new office at my new position. I see that it is a position of prestige and authority. The office is attractive, and the furniture and furnishings are of the best quality. I get up now, and walk out to the reception area. It, too, is attractive and well-appointed. Everything seems new and fresh. The young lady in reception smiles at me as I walk past. The entry doors are large, and as I walk out I see that the building is surrounded by attractive grounds. It is a beautiful work environment. I have a degree of freedom, and I realize that I must be in a senior management role. As I walk back to my office, I sense the respect I receive from others. I am aware that the work is not easy, but it is satisfying, and financially rewarding. My net pay is double what I was receiving before. I return to my desk, and go back to work. I have a smile on my face. I am happy for the first time in a long, long time. I enjoy my new position. I love the challenges, and the fact that it is stretching me. I am learning a great deal, and having an enormous amount of fun in the process.

"I see myself now, visiting Arabella (his former wife) and the boys on the weekend. I take the boys to a baseball game. Afterward, we sit on a beach eating ice creams. On the spur of the moment, I see myself inviting Arabella and the boys out for dinner. We enjoy a beautiful meal in a good restaurant. I can afford the occasional luxury, and it is more satisfying when I do it with the people I love.

"I also see myself walking into Joe Malone's office. I hand him a check. He looks at it with amazement. I tell him I'm sorry it took so long to pay the debt. I see myself leaving his office, with a huge weight lifted off my shoulders. I am free. My debts have all been paid. I am starting to live again.

"I repeat all of these scenes over and over in my mind. It gives me great pleasure to know that they are all going to happen. It hasn't been easy at times, but I can now see the road ahead.

"Thank you for all the blessings in my life. I realize that, compared to many people, I'm leading a good, comfortable life. I am grateful for that, but I want so much more. I want an opportunity to prove myself. I want this for me, my loved ones, the people I owe money to, and for the difference it will make in my life.

"I need this opportunity to double my net income. I can sense it, taste it, feel it. I know that opportunity is out there. I request it now."

(Pause for thirty seconds.) "Thank you. I know my request will be granted. I am now going to return to full conscious awareness on the count of five, confident that my request will be granted. One. Thank you universe. Two. Thanks for all the joys and blessings I already have. Three. I can feel the change in me. Four. Ready for a new start. Five."

You will notice that Josh did not make his request to any specific deity. He requested that the universe provide it for him. If he had had a faith of some sort, it would have been better for him to address his request to that particular deity.

Also, he made a request, rather than a demand. Josh could have demanded the better paying position. When performing a magic ritual, it is common to make a demand. However, Josh felt his petition would work better if he framed it in the form of a request.

This worked, as he got exactly what he asked for. It makes you wonder if he should not have asked for a position that would quadruple his income. This comes down to Josh's self-image and beliefs about himself. Josh needed a miracle, but he still asked for something that he felt was within the realms of possibility. After a year or two, in the new position, he might feel ready to make a request for another doubling of income. If he had started out by requesting a sum that he himself believed to be impossible to achieve, he would have subconsciously sabotaged his efforts, and would have ended up blaming the magic, rather than himself.

Josh visualized himself in a new position, one that satisfied the requirements he had set. He also saw himself enjoying fun times with his children. This scenario involved him doing something that he could not have done without the extra income. The final scene in which he paid off his final debt also was a dramatic one, as it appears that the check he handed over was a sizeable one.

Each of these scenes involved Josh's emotions, as well as his visualization skills. He felt pride and pleasure while sitting behind the desk in his office. He felt love and tenderness with his family. He felt a sense of achievement while paying off his final debt. It is important that emotion is attached to the scenes you visualize, as they have a profound effect on the subconscious mind. Emotions are much more powerful than logic. It is important that positive emotions are involved as much as possible when performing any form of magic. When negative emotions, such as fear and doubt,

creep in, you are much less likely to achieve your goals. Fortunately, your mind can only accommodate one emotion at a time.
Make sure to eliminate any negative emotions before starting any
form of magic.

This has been a brief introduction to magic, one of the most
powerful forces in the universe. In the next several chapters we
will take magic several steps further. You will learn about your
amazing chakra system, and discover how to create miracles with
spell-casting.

Seven

Your Amazing
Chakra System

Y OU ARE MUCH more
than your physical body. You are surrounded
by an invisible energy system, known as the
aura. The aura consists of a number of layers.
The first layer, the one closest to your body, is
called the etheric double. Inside this etheric body,
and expanding outwards, are seven energy centers, or batteries, known as chakras. Although
they are inside the aura, the chakras work har-
moniously with the physical body to keep it acti-
vated, energized and healthy.

The word *chakra* comes from a Sanskrit
word meaning "wheel," as they look like spinning circles of color and energy. They are
sometimes referred to as "wheels of life." Their
task is to absorb, transform, and distribute the
universal life energies throughout the aura.

This universal life energy is known by a variety of names in different cultures. You may be familiar with *prana, ch'i, ki, ankh, ruah,* or *pneuma,* which are all alternative names for the universal life force.

At its most basic this life energy is air, and in the methods of the Kahunas, and also in the meditation exercises, we have seen how important air and the breath are in enabling magic to take place. The universal life energy is your spirit. It is vitally important to every aspect of your life as it looks after your physical, mental and spiritual well-being.

There are seven major chakras. Five are spaced along the spinal column, and the other two are in line with your eyebrows and the top of your head. Each has an important role to play in ensuring that you remain healthy and vibrant. When a chakra is open, you are able to make full use of the qualities that it provides. An open chakra looks something like a lotus, and in the East each chakra is allocated a certain number of petals because of this. When a chakra is closed, or blocked, the universal life energies are not functioning properly in that part of the body, and you will feel a lack of the qual-ities designated by that particular chakra. The fifth chakra, for instance, relates to communication. If that chakra is closed, you would find it hard to express your feelings.

Root Chakra—Muladhara

Color: *Red*

Element: *Earth*

The word *muladhara* comes from *mula,* which means "root," and *adhara,* which means "support." The root, or base, chakra is situated at the base of the spine, in the area of the coccyx. It keeps you grounded, and is concerned with survival. Consequently, matters such as eating, sleeping, earning a living, obtaining shelter, and feeling safe are all concerns of the root chakra. Anything that makes you feel insecure has an effect on your root chakra.

The earth element is associated with this chakra. The earth is solid, substantial, keeps you grounded, and provides you with everything you need to survive. The root chakra draws earth energy up into your body, providing it with energy and strength. This chakra is primarily concerned with your physical body.

When this chakra is balanced, the person feels good about him or herself and the world. He or she will be affectionate, caring, and feel in control. When the root chakra is closed the person will be lacking in confidence and have little motivation or incentive to achieve his or her goals.

Sacral Chakra—Svadhisthana

Color: *Orange*

Element: *Water*

Svadhisthana means "home of the vital force." The sacral chakra is in the lower abdomen, between the navel and the genitals. This chakra is concerned with creativity, sexuality, pleasure, relationships, and the emotions. Because its element is water, it is involved with all the fluid functions of the body, such as circulation, excretion, and sex. When this chakra is balanced, the person is able to express his or her emotions, and has a healthy interest in romance and sexuality. He or she is friendly, positive, and easy to get along with. When it is closed, the person loses contact with his or her emotions, and can be oversensitive, distrustful, and fear-ful. He or she will usually have little interest in sex, but in some cases may recklessly overindulge. Overeating is also common when this chakra is closed.

Solar Plexus Chakra—Manipura

Color: *Yellow*

Element: *Fire*

Manipura means "jewel of the navel." The solar plexus chakra is situated in the lower stomach, slightly above the navel. It repre-sents action, vitality, and personal power, and is also responsible for our metabolism. It processes the emotions, encouraging good, healthy responses, while diluting and neutralizing negative emo-tions. As it relates to the fire element, it provides warmth and energy. Not surprisingly, it is known as the power chakra, as it is the seat of our personal power. When this chakra is balanced the person will feel strong, caring, and able to express his or her feel-ings. He or she will be spontaneous, fun-loving, relaxed, and cheerful. Physical activities will appeal. This person will be able to stand up for him or herself when necessary. His or her emotional life will be full and rich. When the solar plexus chakra is closed the person lacks energy, and will be afraid of confrontation and risks. The negative feelings of worry, insecurity, fear, anger, hate, and depression are common when this chakra is closed.

Heart Chakra—Anahata

Color: *Green*

Element: *Air*

Anahata means "the unstruck sound." The heart chakra is sited in the center of the chest, in the area of the heart. It is the middle chakra, and assists in balancing the three chakras above it, with the three below. Not surprisingly, the heart chakra relates to love, and everything that comes from that. This ranges all the way from simple lust to unconditional love for humanity as a whole. As the heart chakra responds to the air element (prana), it can be opened up and nourished by taking deep breaths. When this chakra is balanced the person will feel contented, and radiate love and compassion. He or she will accept and love him or herself, as well as others. When this chakra is closed, the balance between the top three chakras (mind) and the bottom three (body) is blocked. This creates anxiety, paranoia, and a fear of rejection.

Throat Chakra—Visuddha

Color: *Blue*

Element: *Sound*

Visuddha means "to purify." The throat chakra is situated in the throat. It represents communication, creativity and self-expression, particularly the spoken word. When the throat chakra is balanced the person will be fully at one with him or herself, and able to understand and utilize his or her thoughts and feelings. This person will be creative and find it easy to express him or herself. There is likely to be creative contact with divine energy. When the throat chakra is closed the person will have a fear of expressing him or herself. This sad individual is likely to be timid, quiet, manipulative, and shy. Feelings of depression are common when the throat chakra is closed.

Brow Chakra—Ajna

Color: *Indigo*

Element: *Light*

Ajna means "to know." The brow chakra is situated in the forehead, in the area referred to as the third eye. It relates to our perceptive abilities, visual, as well as intuitive. It looks after your memories, records your dreams, and allows you to look ahead and visualize the future you would like to enjoy. It is concerned with your intuition, providing you with information you could obtain in no other way. When this chakra is balanced the person is able to receive and interpret the insights he or she receives. He or she will be able to develop his or her intuitive capabilities, especially clairvoyance. When the brow chakra is closed, the person is likely to be unassertive, oversensitive, and self-pitying. Physical indications of a blocked brow chakra include headaches, eyestrain, neck pain, and nightmares.

Crown Chakra—Sahasrara

Color: *Violet*

Element: *Thought*

Sahasrara means "thousandfold." The crown chakra is situated immediately above the top of the head, and reaches out into the infinite. It relates to thought, inner wisdom, and the ability to know and understand. It opens the door to universal consciousness and higher awarenesses. In highly evolved people, the brow and crown chakras combine to create a halo. When this chakra is balanced the person is open and receptive to divine energy. When this chakra is closed, the person loses his or her sense of fun and leads a life of pain, disappointment, and frustration, usually accompanied by headaches.

It may appear that the crown chakra is the most important chakra, and the others are merely stepping stones leading to it. In fact, each chakra is just as important as any other. A blockage in any of the chakras is likely to lead to problems elsewhere. In effect, the seven chakras form a spiritual ladder from earth up to heaven, and when they are all balanced and working correctly, we can achieve miracles whenever we wish.

Grounding Yourself with the Chakras

While we are living on this physical plane it is important to remain grounded. This is especially the case when we are working with the higher energies produced by the four uppermost chakras. Fortunately, it is a simple matter to ground ourselves, and you will experience considerable benefit if you perform this exercise at least once a day. You should ground yourself before meditating, or participating in healing work.

Sit down comfortably in a chair with a straight back. Your legs should make a right angle at the knees, and your feet should be resting comfortably on the floor. Take a deep breath, and, as you exhale, push your feet firmly into the floor. You will feel your thigh muscles tighten, and sense a flow of energy into the region of your root chakra. Relax the pressure, then take another deep breath, pushing down with your feet again as you exhale. Do this three or four times, at least once a day, to both energize your root chakra and ground yourself.

Psychic Protection

It is important to protect yourself from negative energies, no matter where it comes from. You can do this by sealing your aura inside a bubble of pure white light.

Sit down comfortably, close your eyes, and take a few slow, deep breaths. Mentally, picture yourself sitting down on a chair in the room you are in. Look at the area around your head and neck and see if you can detect your aura. If not, imagine yourself surrounded by a cocoon-shaped aura.

Take a deep breath in, and watch your aura expand as you fill it up with beneficial prana. See your aura decrease slightly as you exhale. Take a few more breaths to observe your aura increasing and decreasing in size, and then inhale again, this time imagining that you are inhaling the most beautiful red color that you have ever seen. Watch your aura fill up with this beneficial red energy. You might sense the red moving into the area of your root chakra. Exhale slowly, noticing how the red remains inside your aura. Breathe in again, this time noticing that you are inhaling the most gorgeous orange color you have ever seen. Watch it moving into your aura, and sense it in the area of your sacral chakra.

Repeat this five more times, once each with the colors yellow, green, blue, indigo, and violet. Each time you inhale, watch the colors appear in your aura and sense the color moving into their correct chakras.

By the time you have done this, your chakras will be energized and you will be able to see, in your mind's eye, all the colors of the rainbow inside your aura.

You are now ready to add the bubble of protection. Take a few more slow, deep breaths, and then picture a pure white light surrounding your aura. It will start as a slight outline around the aura, but as you watch it, it will form a thicker and denser layer of protective white light around your aura. You can make this protection as large as you wish. I find that six inches of protection is ample for most purposes. If you are living or working with exceptionally negative people, you might want to make it a foot thick. At one time, I worked with a woman who could be described as a psychic vampire. After being in her presence for more than a few minutes I felt drained of energy. I am sure she was not draining other people's energy consciously, but while working with her I kept my white bubble of protection constantly at least one foot wide around my aura.

Balancing Your Chakras

Whenever possible, I prefer to have someone else test and balance my chakras. However, you can do it yourself, if you wish. Many people prefer to balance their own chakras. Experiment with both methods, and see which you prefer. It is a good idea to learn how to balance your own chakras, as every now and again you will find yourself in a situation where there is no one available to do it for you.

Two-Person Method

Stand facing the person you are going to test. This person will usually be slightly tense, so ask him or her to relax before you start. I normally ask the person to shake his or her arms vigorously for a few seconds before starting. Have the person stand, with his or feet slightly apart, and arms by the side.

With your dominant hand and fingers (right hand if you are right-handed, left hand if you are not) disturb the air in the region of the person's crown chakra. Ask the person to extend his arms straight out in front, with the backs of each hand touching. Ask the person to resist what you are going to do. With both hands, grasp the person's wrists and see if you can separate them. There should be a noticeable resistance. If the arms move apart easily, the chakra needs balancing. You can either test all the chakras first, or test and balance, if required, as you work your way down.

The balancing procedure involves the palm of your dominant hand. Hold your palm about an inch away from the chakra that needs balancing, and then start moving your hand in a clockwise motion, forming larger and larger circles as you slowly move back until you are about a yard away from the person. Pause for a few seconds, and then thrust the palm of your hand directly toward the chakra, stopping at about the same position as you started. Test the chakra again. This time the resistance should be much better, indicating that the chakra is now in balance.

Repeat this procedure until all the chakras have been tested, and any that need balancing have been fully charged. Some people prefer to test the person by having him or her lie down, and holding a pendulum over each chakra in turn. If you use this method, you can also use the pendulum to recharge the chakras by deliberately swinging the pendulum in clockwise circles over any chakras that need it.

One-Person Method

This is the method I use when I want to check my chakras but have no one available to assist. All you need to do is ask your pendulum about each chakra in turn, asking if it is in balance. I prefer to ask these questions out loud. Naturally, you will receive a positive response on all the chakras that are in balance, and a negative response on the ones that need attention.

Let's assume that all of your chakras, except for the solar plexus chakra, are in balance. Hold the pendulum and speak directly to the solar plexus chakra. Say something like, "Hello, solar plexus chakra. My pendulum tells me that you are lacking in energy and need to be rebalanced. I am now going to do this with my pendulum." Deliberately swing the pendulum in clockwise circles for fifteen to twenty seconds. Stop the pendulum, and ask it if your solar plexus chakra is now balanced. You can stop at this point, if it gives a positive response. If you receive a negative reply, swing the pendulum in clockwise circles again for a further twenty seconds, while telling your solar plexus chakra what you are doing. Repeat doing this until the pendulum tells you that the chakra is balanced. If you wish, you can go through all of the chakras again to ensure that they are all in balance.

Another method that I enjoy is to take several slow, deep breaths, while visualizing myself inhaling the color that relates to the closed chakra. After filling myself with the desired color in this way, I then use my pendulum to test the chakra again. If it is still weak, I continue breathing in, and absorbing, the desired color until I receive a positive response.

Strengthening Your Chakras

This is an interesting exercise that will fill you with energy and enthusiasm. Start by having a shower or bath. If the weather is warm, allow yourself to dry naturally. Alternatively, rub yourself vigorously all over with a towel. Either skyclad, or wearing a loose-fitting garment, close your eyes and visualize a rapidly spinning circle of red energy in the region of your root chakra. Once you can see it clearly in your mind's eye, visualize a circle of orange energy in the area of your sacral chakra. Move up through each of the chakras in turn, ensuring that you can see the spinning wheel clearly before moving on to the next chakra. As you do this, you are likely to feel the energy of each chakra moving up your spine. After you have visualized a violet circle of energy at your crown chakra, visualize a ray of golden light moving up through your chakras from the root chakra to the crown, spilling over the top and surrounding you in a glorious golden glow. You can send this healing gold light to any part of your body that needs strengthening. Alternatively, you can visualize it gradually dispersing out into the universe to help heal others.

When you feel ready, take a few deep breaths and open your eyes. You will feel totally re-energized and ready for anything after performing this exercise.

This exercise can also be used to change patterns of behavior. You might, for instance, want to stop smoking or lose some weight. You might want to become more relaxed and easy going. You might want to eliminate worry. You might want to start saving money, instead of spending everything you make. It makes no difference what it is that you want to achieve.

Perform the exercise until you see yourself overflowing with the golden glow. Allow this gold to expand until you are inside a huge cocoon of healing gold energy. Think about whatever it is you want to do, and see yourself, the way you want to be, inside the cocoon of gold. If you want to stop smoking, for instance, do not think, "I want to stop smoking." Instead, say, "I am a nonsmoker." You need to think about the accomplishment, rather than what you need to do. Similarly, you would say, "My weight will be __ pounds," rather than "I want to lose thirty pounds."

Repeat this exercise every day until you achieve your goal.

Bedtime Restoration Exercise

This is a pleasant exercise that strengthens your chakras, and also ensures that you enjoy a good night's sleep. You will need to obtain some swatches of the seven colors of the rainbow. I was fortunate, as I found a gift set of seven silk handkerchiefs, one each of all the colors necessary. At bedtime, do not immediately snuggle between the sheets. Start by lying on top of the bed, and place a swatch of the correct color on the area of each chakra. Close your eyes and think about the day you have just experienced. Think about the good things that happened during the day. They do not have to be major incidents. If someone smiled at you when you passed them in the street, include that. Think of anything that made you feel happy.

Once you have done that, turn your mind to the less enjoyable aspects of your day. As you think about each one, allow your body to let you know which chakra was affected. You may experience a sensation of some sort, or possibly experience a sense of knowing which chakra it was. Think of the swatch of color lying over this chakra, and allow the energies of the color to spread into your body. When you feel ready, let go of the negative incident, and go on to the next one. Repeat the procedure until you have covered all of the negative experiences of the day. Once you have done this, direct your attention to each chakra in turn, starting at the root chakra, and allowing the color from the swatch to fill the chakra with energy. When you have done this, remove the swatches, get between the sheets, and allow yourself to drift off to sleep. We all experience unpleasantness and negativity as we go through life. It is extremely healing to deal with it before going to sleep, and this exercise allows you to strengthen each of the chakras at the same time.

If you do not have any swatches of the right colors, you can still do this exercise by imagining they are there. I prefer to do it with the swatches of color, but find that imagining them works just as well.

Accomplishing Miracles with Chakras

Your chakras are the most important psychic centers in your body. When they are harmonized and in perfect balance, you can use their enormous power to achieve your goals. Imagine the unbelievable power you possess when you harness these seven powerful centers of energy and focus them on a single desire.

The method used is similar to the one for strengthening your chakras. The main difference is that you will be using that energy to achieve a specific goal. Start by relaxing comfortably in a place where you will not be disturbed. You can either lie down, or sit in a comfortable chair for this exercise.

Start by taking a few slow, deep breaths. Close your eyes and allow all of the muscles of your body to relax. When you feel totally relaxed, focus on your root chakra. Imagine that your conscious-ness is in this area, and visualize the chakra as a whirling circle of red energy that supports and revitalizes your entire being. When you feel a warmth, tingle, or other sensation in this area, move your attention to your sacral chakra, and follow the same process there. Once you feel a sensation in this area, move up to the next chakra until you have worked your way up to the crown chakra. When you feel your crown chakra tingling with vitality and energy, think of your goal. Picture the exact wording of whatever it is you desire on a huge billboard or movie screen. When you can clearly visualize this in your mind, feel the energy in all of the chakras, silently read the words on the billboard, and say to yourself, "That is what I want. I am attracting it to me now." Hold the feeling of success for as long as you can, and, when it starts to fade, let it go.

Relax quietly for a few minutes once you have done this. You do not need to continue thinking about your request. You have sent it out into the universe, and a response will come in due course. Enjoy pleasant thoughts for a few minutes, and then open your eyes. Repeat this exercise at least three times a week, and preferably daily, until your request is granted.

Sometimes a response comes almost immediately, while at other times you need a great deal of patience. Be alert to what is going on in your life while you are waiting for a response. Sometimes the results can come in strange, almost hidden, ways.

Eight

Spell-Casting

WHEN YOU WERE a child you probably believed that people could cast spells and create real magic as a result. However, as you grew up you may have discarded these ideas, thinking they were too far-fetched, childish, or impossible. This is a shame because everyone has the ability to cast spells. The results of successful spell-casting can be miraculous.

Whenever you perform a spell, you draw on the hidden powers of your mind to influence the outer world and bring to you whatever it is you desire. Four factors are necessary: someone or something to invoke, visualization, concentration, and symbolism.

You start by visualizing the goal in your mind. You must be able to feel it, sense it, see it, hear it, and almost even taste it. You must be absolutely certain in your mind that this desire will become a reality, and that everyone will benefit as a result.

You then need to invoke an appropriate source of power who you hope will make the spell come true. If you come from a Christian background, you will probably invoke God. Alternatively, you might invoke the architect of the universe, or Pan, Athena, Isis, or any other god. Whenever you say grace you are performing a blessing spell. You start by invoking God, and then give thanks for the meal that you are about to eat. Spells work in exactly the same way. In fact, most prayers could be described as spells. Unfortunately, most people pray as a last resort, which means their minds are filled with fear and dread. When these emotions are passed on to the universal mind, it is most unlikely that the prayer will be answered, as the negative emotions are all that gets through. If you pray, using the four factors of invocation, visualization, concentration, and symbolism, and add a healthy amount of belief, your prayers will be answered every time, as you will have created a perfect spell.

You need to concentrate on your desire while performing the spell. It is important that you remain firmly focused on this desire until the spell has been completed.

Symbolism is necessary to represent the people or situation involved in the spell. You can use almost anything for this, as long as it is clear to you what everything you are using symbolizes. You can use colors, scents, photographs, drawings, words on paper, personal items, and anything else that happens to appeal to you. Nail clippings and locks of hair are usually found in fairy stories, but can be used if you wish. I tend to avoid using anything that belongs, or has belonged, to someone else, without receiving permission from the person first. Consequently, I am always given something better than a nail clipping or strand of hair.

The Four Elements

At least one of the four traditional elements are used when casting a spell. This is because each of them has symbolic associations with various aspects of human life. Also, they all combine to form spirit, which could be considered a fifth element. It is this spirit that enables us to harness the unseen forces and achieve our goals.

Fire

The Fire element relates to passion, energy, strength, vitality, enthusiasm, motivation, and anything involving action and forward progress.

Earth

The Earth element relates to stability, endurance, steadiness, strength, growth, perseverance, and healing. It also relates to the home, fertility, children, pets, and family life.

Air

The Air element relates to creativity, the arts, imagination, mental stimulation, and the intellect. It also relates to travel, both physically and astrally.

Water

The Water element relates to the emotions, love, fertility, fruit-fulness, harmony, and cooperation. It also relates to dreaming, meditation, intuition, divination, death, and rebirth.

Love and Money

Throughout the ages, most spells have been concerned with love and prosperity. Everyone wants to love and be loved, and every-one, no matter how rich, wants more wealth. There are particular colors that relate to love and money. Pink symbolizes love, and red represents passion. Friday is generally considered the best day for love spells. This is because Friday is related to Venus, the god-dess of love. Green is the color to use to attract money. Thursday is a good day for spells involving money, as Jupiter is the god of expansion, and Thursday is his day.

You need to be particularly careful with love spells. You can cast a spell to attract love, but you must not do it to make yourself more attractive to a particular person. This is known as a bidding spell, in which you ask for what you want, but pay no attention to the desires or free will of others. You might be desperately in love with someone in your office, but if he or she shows no interest in you, you can not cast a spell to make yourself more attractive to that person. All of your spells must be pure, hurt no one, and ide-ally benefit as many people as possible.

Healing Spells

Spells can be used to help heal others, assuming that they want to be healed. With healing spells it is usual for an object, such as a crystal, to be charged and energized in the course of the spell. This object is kept close to the sick person until he or she is well again.

Blessing Spells

We have already mentioned grace as a spell of blessing. Blessing spells are special spells in which thanks is given for benefits that have been received, or are being received. You might give thanks that you, or someone close to you, has returned to good health after an illness. You might give thanks for peace of mind, a job promotion, an unexpected windfall, or anything else that you are grateful for. If you have somehow miraculously escaped danger, you should make a spell of thanks. You might give thanks for something on an international level, such as the ending of a war. You can give thanks for events that occur on a local level, such as the election of a mayor, or the opening of a new facility that will benefit the community. You need never run out of things to be thankful about.

It is a good habit to perform blessing spells regularly. Many spells are performed for what could be considered selfish reasons, so it is good to perform a spell of thanks every now and again to demonstrate that you are concerned about the well being of others, as well as yourself.

Creating Spells

A large part of the enjoyment of spell-casting comes from devising a suitable spell to send out to the universe. Here are a couple of examples.

Spell to Attract a Lover

Required: one red candle, two sheets of white paper, red marking pen, an envelope, and a wine glass containing red wine (or colored water, if preferred).

Elements used: Fire from the candle. This symbolizes energy, enthusiasm and passion. Water from the wine. This symbolizes love and romance.

Best time to perform the spell: Friday, ideally when the moon is waxing.

Start by gathering the items you need, and placing them on your altar. After this, enjoy a relaxing bath or shower. Do not rush this stage. Make it as luxurious and pleasurable as possible. You might want to use bath salts, and listen to romantic music while in the bath. Dry yourself with a good-quality, clean towel. Change into clean, loose-fitting clothes, or alternatively work skyclad.

Return to your altar and place the candle at the back of the altar. In front of this, place the two sheets of paper. The wine glass should be on the right-hand-side of the altar.

Stand, or sit, in front of your altar, light the candle, and then ask for the blessing of whichever deity you wish. As you are casting a spell for love, you might want to ask Venus to help you attain your goal.

Pause for a few moments after invoking the deity. Then write down on one of the pieces of paper a rhyming couplet that depicts your goal. This does not have to be great poetry. No one is going to see it, except you. It is far more effective to create a couplet for yourself, rather than using something you may have read somewhere. "Rain, rain, go away, come again another day" may well have been used as a spell at one time, but no one seriously expects it to work nowadays, as it has become tired and over-used. Write something fresh and original. You might write something along these lines:

"I seek a lover to make my life complete,
Please come to me quickly, so we can meet."

Write the couplet slowly and deliberately. Once you have written it, read it out loud three times. Fold the sheet of paper into quarters and place it on your altar directly in front of the candle.

Draw a large heart on the second sheet of paper. Color it in with the red marker. Sip the wine until the glass is empty. As you do this, visualize yourself being filled with passion and enormous reserves of energy.

Hold the heart over the candle flame for a few moments, and then fold it and place it in the envelope. Use wax from the candle to seal it shut. Place this envelope at the front of your altar.

Pick up the folded sheet of paper containing the rhyming couplet. Read it out loud three times, putting as much energy and enthusiasm into your voice as possible. Fold the paper again, and then burn it in the candle flame. As it burns, visualize your request going out into the universe, where it will be acted upon.

Thank the deity you invoked at the start of the ceremony. Snuff out the candle, and place the envelope somewhere where it will not be seen or disturbed by others. Allow it to remain there for twenty-eight days, one full cycle of the Moon. If the universe has not brought you a lover by this time, burn the envelope, and perform the entire ritual again.

Remember that you are performing a spell of attraction, in this case a spell to attract a lover. The universe will do its best to provide you with whatever it is you ask for, but you also need to play your part. You will have to go out and meet people during the next four weeks. Accept every social invitation that comes your way, as you never know which one he or she will be at. Pay particular attention to everyone you meet during this time. You might meet your lover accidentally while travelling to or from work, or while shopping. If you spend all your evenings and weekends at home, you are most unlikely to meet your lover, no matter how many spells you cast.

Money Attraction Spell

Required: One green candle, two sheets of paper, an envelope, green marking pen, a small metal container, seven quarters, and a glass of red wine (or colored water).

Elements: All four.

Best time to perform this spell: Any Thursday, or the night of the New Moon.

Start by placing the necessary items on your altar, and then enjoy a relaxing shower or bath. Indulge yourself. Use good-quality soaps and fragrances. Spend as long as you wish in the bath. Dry yourself with a clean, good-quality towel, and then put on clean, loose-fitting garments. Naturally, you can also work sky-clad, if desired.

Return to your altar and place the green candle at the back of your altar, in the center. Place the two sheets of paper in front of the candle, and put the glass of wine on your right-hand side. Place the metal container on your left-hand side, with the quarters arranged in a row immediately in front of it.

Stand, or sit, in front of the altar. Light the candle, and gaze into the flame for sixty seconds, before invoking whichever deity you wish. You might choose Jupiter, as you are requesting a financial increase. Pause for a minute or two, until you feel the presence of the deity in the room.

When you feel ready, write on the first sheet of paper the exact amount of money you desire. Make this figure as high as you dare, but the sum must not be more than you believe you can request and receive. You can test the amount by closing your eyes, and saying to yourself, "I deserve x number of dollars." Pause until you feel a response in your body. If the response is excited and positive, you have chosen a good sum to ask for. If the response is negative and you feel scared or anxious, lower the sum and try again. If you feel no response at all, raise the sum as many times as necessary, until you feel a positive response.

Once you have written down the desired amount of money, write down a rhyming couplet that relates to your request. You might write something like:

"Money comes in silver and gold,
I need it now, not when I'm old."

Recite your couplet three times. Once you have done this, hold the sheet of paper in front of the candle, so that you can read the numbers and the rhyme you have written, and also see the outline of the flame behind it. Fold this sheet of paper into four, and place it on your altar immediately in front of the candle.

On the second sheet of paper draw a picture of whatever it is you will be doing with the money, once you receive it. If you plan buying a new car, draw a car. If you intend paying bills, draw a picture of you handing the money over to the person or persons you owe. You might draw several things, depending on the amount you have asked for, and what you want to do. Your artistic skills are unimportant, as no one will see what you have drawn, anyway.

Pick up the glass of wine, and slowly sip it, while looking at your drawing. Think of what you will do with the money once you receive it.

Put down the empty wine glass, and pick up the metal container. Pick up one of the quarters and drop it into the container, saying out loud, "I attract wealth and abundance." Repeat this until all of the quarters have been placed into the container. Replace this container on your left-hand side.

Write on the bottom, right-hand corner of the sheet of paper containing your drawing the word "Fire." As you do this, say out loud, "I need all the vitality, energy, and enthusiasm that the Fire element can give me."

Write "Earth" on the bottom, left-hand corner. As you write it, say out loud, "I need the wisdom, stability, and patience that the Earth element can give me."

Write "Air" two-thirds of the way up the right-hand side of the sheet of paper. Say, "I need all of the creative insights, imagination, and brain power that the Air element can give me."

Write "Water" two-thirds of the way up the left-hand side of the paper. Say, "I need all of the emotional stability, cooperation, harmony, and universal love that the Water element can give me."

Write "Spirit" at the top of the sheet of paper, in the center. Say, "I need all of the power, energy, and accomplishment that Spirit can provide."

(The five elements represent a symbolic pentagram, or five-pointed star. The pentagram is an ancient magical symbol that unifies the elements, and adds power to the spell.)

Look at the sheet of paper, and repeat the statements about each of the elements. Try to feel the sensation each one has on your physical body. Fold this sheet of paper and place it in the envelope, sealing it with wax from the candle.

Pick up the folded sheet of paper. Open it, and read the sum of money you have written on it out loud. Use as much enthusiasm and energy as you can. Recite the rhyming couplet three times. Fold the sheet of paper, and then burn it in the candle flame. As it burns, visualize your request going out into the universe and being granted.

Thank whichever deity you invoked at the start of the ritual. Snuff out the candle. Place the envelope in a safe place where it will not be disturbed, but where you will see it several times a day. Place the container of coins on top of it.

Every day for seven days, empty the quarters out and drop them back into the container one at a time, saying, "I attract wealth and abundance" each time. After seven days, give the coins away. This serves to emphasize the fact that your fortunes are increasing and you no longer need them.

In both of these examples, we have created a ritual out of the spell. I enjoy performing them this way, as I feel the emotional energy that is created helps the whole process. However, rituals and spells can be done separately. Many magicians perform spells by gathering together the necessary ingredients in one place, and allowing the objects to create the magic.

It may seem hard to believe that simply grouping a few items together can create a miracle. To ensure success you must believe that it is possible. Although, in this instance, you are not performing a ceremony of any sort, your belief in the outcome allows the universal forces to act on your desire and make it happen. You express this to the world while gathering the necessary items, and you imbue yourself, the items, and the area the objects are in with the necessary energy to enable the spell to work.

You could, for instance, perform a money attraction spell with a dollar bill, a few coins, and a metal container. Wrap the coins inside the dollar bill and place the packet inside the container. Place the container somewhere where you will see it several times a day. Every time you notice it, say to yourself, "I attract wealth and abundance."

This is very similar to the silent affirmations that are used in the East. Thousands of years ago, silent motivations were used to motivate the people. They noticed that some fish, for instance, swam up rivers and even leaped up waterfalls, to reach the breeding grounds. Consequently, fish came to mean upward progress, which was important in a society in which success was determined by a person's ability to pass the official exams. More than thirty years ago, when I first started visiting the Far East, I was fascinated with the metal containers containing a few coins that I frequently saw on people's desks. This was a silent affirmation to remind the person what he or she was doing at work, and to attract more money.

Spells can also consist of specific words that relate to whatever it is that is desired. "Give us this day our daily bread" could be considered a spell. Most affirmations are a form of spell-casting. Reciting a special mantra is also creating a spell. Some nursery rhymes began as spells. How about this one that is used for luck:

"Ladybug, ladybug, fly away home.
Your house is afire and your children alone."

Bedtime prayers are actually spells of protection. Here are two favorite prayers that have been used for generations:

"Now I lay me down to sleep.
I pray The Lord my soul to keep.
If I should die before I wake,
I pray The Lord my soul to take."

"Matthew, Mark, Luke, and John,
Bless the bed that I lie on."

I am sure you are familiar with the saying: "Something old, something new, something borrowed, something blue." However, did you know that the original spell contained an extra line: "And a sprig of furze." Could this explain the failure of so many marriages?

Not every spell works. When this happens, you need to examine what you said and did to find out where you went wrong. Perhaps your need was not as great as you thought it was. Maybe the outcome you desired was not expressed clearly enough. It is possible that your spell might have inadvertently affected someone else. Maybe your circumstances had changed and the outcome was no longer as important as you had thought. Maybe you subconsciously failed to believe that the spell would work. Think about these things, and if you still desire the outcome, create another spell for yourself.

Finally, what do you do if you think someone has put a spell on you? This person is practicing spell-binding, which is a negative form of magic. There are two traditional methods to eliminate the effects of this. The first is to blow on your fingers. The second method can only be used if you know who has cast the spell. Make a "fig" with your hand. You do this by making a fist, and then inserting your thumb between your first two fingers, so that it protrudes slightly in front of the fingers. The figa, or fig, is a commonly used way of averting the evil eye. Point the figa at whoever you think has put a spell on you, while silently saying to yourself, "The spell no longer has any hold on me. I am free." Other traditional remedies are to cross your fingers, make a sign of the cross, or spit on the ground while telling yourself the spell no longer has any effect on you.

Nine

Automatic Writing

THERE WILL BE times when you know exactly what you want, while on other occasions you may have no idea at all. Many times people have said to me, "I don't know what's going on. I need a miracle." Obviously, something is going on in their lives that they have not been able to identify. It might be a vague feeling of dissatisfaction, or a concern that they are not progressing with their lives.

Fortunately, there is a useful technique to obtain the missing information from our unconscious minds. The technical term for it is psychography, but it is better known as automatic writing. If you have ever doodled while talking to someone on the phone, you will have experienced a form of automatic writing.

When you doodle, the drawings appear effortlessly, with little or no conscious input. Some people create drawings that are much better than anything they could do consciously.

Automatic writing is similar to this. The person allows him- or herself to enter an almost trancelike state, which allows the writing arm and hand to move with what seems to be a mind of its own. Sometimes the words that appear can surprise the person who unconsciously wrote them, especially if they express views that he or she normally opposes.

Anyone can learn how to do automatic writing. All you need to do is hold a pen in your writing hand, and enter the correct frame of mind. Some people are able to distract themselves completely while writing in this way. They may watch television or enjoy a conversation, while the pen they are holding writes by itself. Some people remain aware of what they are writing, as the pen writes, but have no idea what the next words will be.

Patience is required. When you first start experimenting with this, you are likely to produce scribbles or letters that mean nothing. However, with practice, you will surprise yourself with what you produce. Some people produce automatic writing in so tiny a script that a magnifying glass is required to read it. Some people produce mirror writing. There have even been cases of people writing in languages that they were not familiar with. One well-documented example of this was Hélène Smith, a nineteenth-century Swiss medium. She was able to automatically write in Arabic.[1] Some people produce words slowly, but there have been many documented cases of people producing well over a thousand words an hour while automatic writing. The Reverent Vale Owen was able to write approximately twenty-four words a minute, four nights a week, for months on end. His average speed was 1,440 words an hour.[2]

A huge amount of work, some of an extremely high standard, has been produced by automatic writing. Much channeled information has arrived this way. Madame Blavatsky and Alice Bailey both stated that much of their published works had come from sources outside themselves.[3] Harriet Beecher Stowe, author of *Uncle Tom's Cabin*, said that she did not write the book, but that it was given to her. William Blake wrote that his famous poem, "Jerusalem," was dictated to him, and he merely wrote it down. In his preface, William Blake wrote: "I may praise it, since I dare not pretend to be other than the Secretary; the authors are in eternity."

Even parts of the Bible were transmitted through automatic writing. In 2 Chronicles 21:12, we read: "And there came a writing to him from Elijah the prophet, saying, Thus saith the Lord God of David thy father."

In 1852, Reverend C. Hammond's book, *The Pilgrimage of Thomas Payne and Others to the Seventh Circle*, became the first work produced entirely by automatic writing to be published in the United States. This book of 250 pages took just over a month to be received. Many other works, largely of a spiritual nature, followed. *Oahspe*, a cosmic Bible received by Dr. John Ballou Newbrough in 1882, is still readily available in New Age stores. It is possibly the first book to be received by automatic typewriting. Ruth Montgomery is a recent example of an author who wrote a series of books using automatic typewriting.[4] Alfred, Lord Tennyson,

William Butler Yeats, and Gertrude Stein are three examples of well known authors who used automatic writing to expand their creativity. In his autobiography, *Something of Myself*, Rudyard Kipling wrote: "the pen took charge, and I watched it begin to write stories about Mowgli and animals, which later grew into *The Jungle Books*."5 In his preface to a book created by automatic writing, the philosopher C. H. Broad wrote: "There is, undoubtedly, some independent evidence for the existence, in some few persons, of remarkable creative and dramatizing powers, which reveal themselves only when their possessor is in a dissociated state."6

By far the most famous examples of automatic writing are those attributed to Patience Worth, who communicated through a Ouija board. The Ouija board as we know it today was invented by Elijah J. Bond and William Fuld in 1892. This is a board containing the letters of the alphabet in two curved rows, a row of numbers from one to zero, and the words "yes," "no," and "goodbye" printed on it. The planchette, a small triangular or heart-shaped plate with wheels or ball bearings on two corners, and a pencil on the third, was invented by M. Planchette, a French spiritualist, in 1853.7 Nowadays, planchettes usually have three felt pads, instead of wheels and a pencil, on each corner. However, variations of the planchette and Ouija boards have been around for a long time. In 540 BCE, Pythagoras conducted séances in which a special table on wheels moved toward different signs, in much the same way that a planchette moves on a Ouija board. This is a form of automatic writing.

In 1913, two young women in St. Louis began experimenting with a Ouija board. Most of the early messages they received were unimportant, but on the night of July 8, the board spelled out: "Many moons ago I lived. Again I come. Patience Worth is my name."

The two women, twenty-one-year-old Pearl Curran and friend Emily Hutchings, were amazed, especially when the planchette started moving again. This time it spelled out: "Wait. I would speak with thee. If thou shalt live, then so shall I. I make my bread by thy hearth. Good friends, let us be merrie. The time for work is past. Let the tabbie drowse and blink her wisdom to the fire-log."

Pearl and Emily immediately began asking the Ouija board questions about Patience Worth. They discovered that she was an English Quaker who had lived in the seventeenth century. She proved to be so charming and amusing, that the two women began recording every message that came through.

Once Patience Worth started communicating, she proved to be highly prolific, and six novels, several plays, and more than four thousand poems were dictated, letter by letter, through the Ouija board. An anthology of the "best" poetry of 1917 included five poems by Patience Worth, two more than were included by Amy Lowell and Vachel Lindsay, leading poets of the day.

The quality of Patience Worth's work was excellent. The New York Times described one of her books as "remarkable." The *London Evening Standard* said that her novel, *Hope Trueblood*, was "worthy of Dickens at his best."

Pearl Curran found that as long as she had contact with the planchette, Patience Worth would come through. Anyone else could touch the planchette at the same time, but the messages

undoubtedly came through Pearl. After using the Ouija board for
several years, Pearl discovered that she could simply speak the letters while a friend wrote them down.

Not surprisingly, Patience Worth had her share of doubters.
This did not worry her in the least, and she regularly made jokes
about them. She even composed a poem for the people who insisted
that she prove that she was real:

> A phantom? Well enough
> Prove thee thyself to be.
> I say, behold, here I be—
> Buskins, kirtle, cap, and pettyskirts,
> And much tongue.
> Weel, what hast thou to prove thee?[8]

In 1908, Frederick Bligh Bond (1863–1945) was in charge of
the excavations at Glastonbury Abbey. A year earlier, he had
enlisted the aid of his friend, Captain John Bartlett (1863–1933),
a well-known medium, songwriter, and retired ship's officer in an
experiment in cooperative automatic writing. He placed his hand
on top of Bartlett's and asked: "Can you tell us anything about
Glastonbury Abbey?" The information that came through was
amazing. John Bartlett used automatic writing to contact the
spirit of a medieval monk named Johannes Bryant, who was able
to tell Bond exactly where to find the missing Edgar Chapel and
the remains of a destroyed shrine. The automatic writing was a
mixture of Middle English and Latin.[9] John Bartlett also produced
a number of drawings of Glastonbury Abbey in the same manner.
This is known as automatic drawing. It is interesting to note that

he did these with his left hand, even though he wrote with his right hand.

W. T. Stead (1849–1912) was a well-known journalist and human rights campaigner who used automatic writing extensively. On one occasion, Stead was getting ready to meet a friend at a railway station. The friend had said that her train would arrive at "about three." Before leaving for the station, Stead mentally asked his friend to take control of his hand and give a more accurate time for the train's arrival. The automatic writing said the train would arrive at ten to three. Stead went to the station and found the train had been delayed. He took pencil and paper from his pocket and asked his friend: "Why the mischief have you been so late?" He received the following response: "We were detained at Middlesborough for so long; I do not know why." The train arrived shortly afterwards, and Stead asked his friend why it was late. "I do not know," she replied. "The train stopped so long at Middlesborough, it seemed as if it would never start."[10]

Experimenting with Automatic Writing

The best way to start automatic writing is to experiment in a carefree, lighthearted manner. If you sit at a table, grimly determined to receive a message, nothing is likely to happen. However, if you sit down, with an attitude that it doesn't matter if anything comes through or not, you are more likely to achieve success.

Sit down with your writing arm, creating a ninety-degree angle at the elbow. The hand holding the pen or pencil should rest comfortably on a pad of paper. Relax as much as possible and see what happens. Many people like to close their eyes and withdraw into a quiet, meditative state at this stage. You might like to deliberately relax every muscle in your body, as we have done with some of the other techniques in this book. The more relaxed you are, the better. I have met several people who silently say positive affirmations about automatic writing at this stage. You might say: "I am now relaxed and receptive to any messages that come through. I know the information will be helpful to me in my daily life, and I am ready and willing to receive."

After a while, the hand holding the writing instrument will start to move. Resist the temptation to look at what is happening. Automatic writing is unconscious writing, and any conscious interest will immediately stop the flow of the writing.

If you are fortunate, you will start writing words and sentences right away. Most people start with circles, ellipses and illegible shapes. You may produce a word or two in mirror writing. It makes no difference what the pen produces in the first few sessions. As long as you have drawn something you have made a good start. There will be occasions, even once you've become an expert, when nothing will come through. This means that nothing is available to be transcribed at that time. Put your writing implements away, and try again later.

It seems a simple matter to place the tip of a pencil on a sheet of paper, enter into a relaxed, meditative state, and then relax while the pencil writes out messages. For many people, it is just this simple. However, some people find it hard to get started.

Try resting the point of your pen or pencil on the sheet of paper, making sure your hand and wrist make no contact with the table. Your arm will soon become tired, and the pen will start to move.

Experiment with holding the pen in different ways. I have seen people automatic writing while holding the pen in their clenched fists. I also know someone who holds the pen between his first two fingers. You might find that these variations work well for you.

You might try writing with your other hand. I have had no success with this myself, but many people find that automatic writing is easier when the non-dominant hand is used. I have been told that anyone can learn to do automatic writing with either hand. However, you are more likely to mirror-write with your less dominant hand than you are with the hand you normally write with.

Another method is to start the pencil moving by drawing large circles on the sheet of paper. Once you have started, pay no further attention to the movements of your hand. Frequently, the pencil, once started in this manner, will gradually stop drawing circles and will start automatic writing.

Many people sense a tingling sensation in their hand just before the pen starts moving. A few people experience a profound jerking sensation, followed by the pen taking on a life of its own. I have neither seen nor experienced this myself. The Reverend Stainton Moses (1839–1892), a well-known nineteenth-century Spiritualist had a violent start to automatic writing in 1872: "My right arm was seized about the middle of the forearm, and dashed violently up and down with a noise resembling that of a number of paviors at work. It was the most tremendous exhibition of 'unconscious muscular action' I ever saw. In vain I tried to stop it. I distinctly felt the grasps, soft and firm, round my arm, and though perfectly possessed of senses and volition, I was powerless to interfere, although my hand was disabled for some days by the bruising it then got. The object we soon found was to bring up the force."[11]

You will find that the best results occur if you experiment with automatic writing at the same time every day. I find that the best time for me is in the evening when I'm starting to feel tired. At this time it is easy to slip into the right state of mind. A partially darkened room is also helpful. Another benefit I found from practicing at the same time each day, is that the messages usually carry on from those received on the previous day.

Practice as often as possible. Stop whenever you feel tired, or when the writing appears to have stopped. There is nothing to be gained by forcing yourself to sit at a table for hours on end, producing nothing. Fifteen or twenty minutes every day will produce results much more quickly than a two-hour session once a week.

With regular practice you'll be amazed at what you produce. You will find that you can write for hours on end without becoming physically tired. Everyone is different. Some people can do automatic writing while watching television or chatting with friends. I knew someone who could read a book while producing automatic writing. Some people prefer to sit quietly in a meditative state while their writing hand records the information that is coming through. Experiment, and find which method you prefer. You will find that the quality of the information coming through will improve the more you practice.

There is no limit to what you might produce. You will receive information about your past, present, and future. Automatic writing may well increase your latent creativity. You might create poems, novels, plays, or receive answers to questions that are troubling you. You can even receive replies for other people's questions, and receive further details about dreams you may have experienced. Often our dreams speak to us in symbols that are hard to understand. Frequently, dream symbols have a variety of possible interpretations, and it is important to find out which one is correct. None of this is a problem to our unconscious minds. You can use automatic writing to answer any questions you may have about your dreams.

Once you become proficient at automatic writing you can ask your unconscious mind anything you wish. You might, for instance, ask: "Do I deserve a miracle in my life?" Obviously, the answer to this question will have a bearing on everything else that is covered in this book. If you receive a negative reply, you will obviously have to ask more questions to find out why your unconscious mind does not consider you worthy. Work on the replies you receive, and then ask the question again. Keep on doing this until you receive a positive response.

You can ask questions about anything that is going on in your life. Should you ask a certain person out? Put pen to paper and find out. Should you make a certain investment? Take a vacation? Accept an invitation? Change jobs? What would be the best career choice for me? You can ask general questions, such as "What should I know about my future?" and specific questions, such as: "Where are my car keys?" There is no limit to what you can ask.

Your unconscious mind knows much more than you can possibly imagine. Normally, access to it is limited. However, because automatic writing is not screened and censored by the conscious mind, it provides a direct link to all the information stored there. Consequently, you can ask it anything at all. Developing the skill of automatic writing enables you to access this information whenever you wish. That, in itself, is a miracle.

Ten

Conclusion

YOU NOW KNOW everything you need to create your own miracles. From now on you will not be able to blame bad luck if you feel that you're not progressing in life. If you are unhappy with any aspect of your life, you will be able to make the necessary changes by listening to your inner mind. You have the ability to turn your life around, and achieve virtually anything you wish. Naturally, you need to set a goal, invoke a higher power, work hard, remain motivated, and then create a miracle.

You must also be prepared to accept it. Strangely enough, not everyone is willing to accept a miracle. Jesus was unable to perform miracles when he went back to Nazareth, as the inhabitants were not prepared to accept them (Matthew 13: 54–58). Because of their unbelief,

Jesus was unable to heal them. Consequently, to receive miracles in your own life, you must be prepared to accept them.

Miracles occur in a variety of ways. For a disabled person, a miracle would most likely be a sudden healing that made him or her whole again. However, another example of a miracle might be for that person to somehow learn to consider the disability as a learning experience. Once that person accepted the situation, and made the best of it, he or she could make enormous progress in this incarnation. Is the second scenario any less miraculous than the first?

The fact that you are alive and reading this book is a miracle. The concept that life itself is a miracle is a comfort to many, and enables them to make sense of their lives. They can trust in the order of the world, and believe that everything will work out exactly the way in which the creator planned it. For them, miracles need no explanation and reveal God's presence in everything.

Aldous Huxley described this point of view extremely well:

Thankfulness for the privilege of being alive and a witness to this miracle, of being, indeed, more than a witness—a partner in it. Thankfulness for these gifts of luminous bliss and knowledgeless understanding. Thankfulness for being at once this union with the divine unity and yet this finite creature among other finite creatures.[1]

If you look back over your life, you will probably remember incidents that you considered to be either coincidence or luck. If you examine them closely, you may find that they were, in fact, miracles. Many miracles are unrecognized. You need to be prepared, willing to receive, and remain positively expectant. This will help you develop what *New Age Journal* editor Marc Barasch calls a "miracle-prone personality."[2]

Every aspect of your life will become more joyful when you choose to live each day with a sense of the miraculous. There is no need to give away all your possessions and become a monk or hermit. When you lead your life in such a way that you feel fulfilled, and in your own way are making a difference to the world, you allow the spiritual side of your nature to develop and grow, and will gain a true sense of who you are. In every type of situation you will show your true nature. You will be "in the flow" and every aspect of your life will become miraculous.

Just imagine enjoying every day free of stress and negativity, totally at peace, in control, and achieving everything that needs to be done. You do not need to be a minister or rabbi to lead a spiritual life. You can express your spiritual nature in everything you do, no matter what your occupation.

One of the most successful people I ever met was a road sweeper who worked in the red light district of the city I live in. He took pride in his work, and it showed. He smiled at everyone, and regularly counseled people who were feeling low. He ultimately wrote a book about his life as a road sweeper. The spiritual side of his nature was apparent in everything he did. It makes no difference what work you do. If you perform it in a spiritually loving way, you will enjoy the rich rewards that come from this approach to life, and will open yourself up to the miraculous in everyday life.

You can do this in both small and large ways. It is usually better to start with modest goals and build on your successes. Ultimately, you might reach the level achieved by Dr. Philip S. Bailey, a San Francisco dentist. He became fascinated with miracles that involved duplication of food. He had studied religion and intuition, and felt that the miracles he had read about were achieved by the psychic abilities of Jesus and other great prophets. These wonder workers were highly sensitive and highly intuitive. Because he considered himself psychic, also, he began a series of experiments. The first thing he noticed was that a store of oranges he had placed in a cupboard increased in number. He then noticed that the stack of firewood he kept by the fireplace was also increasing. After these initial discoveries, he began more formal experiments. In one of these, he prepared ten slices of apple and seven slices of bread for his wife and a guest. By the time he had taken them to the dining room, the bread had increased to eight slices. Both people ate two slices of apple each, and Mrs. Haley had two pieces of bread.

When the food was counted again, they discovered they still had nine pieces of apple and seven slices of bread. Dr. Haley performed more than twenty successful experiments of this sort. Many of them were witnessed by others. Dr. Haley recorded his miracles in a book called *Modern Loaves and Fishes and Other Studies in Psychic Phenomena*.[3] Incidentally, one of the messages of Dr. Haley's book was that no one religion controls the ability to perform miracles. He believed that it was a natural human phenomenon that anyone could learn to do.

Once you start achieving success in these areas, you should contemplate the incredible results that could be obtained when a group of like-minded people get together. You, and your colleagues, could perform a miracle that would benefit humanity as a whole. Start small, on your own, and then progress further and further. There are no limits to how far you could go.

Of course you should ask for miracles in your life. You should do so regularly. Ask for both small and big miracles. Doing this will help you realize most of your goals. It is not good to achieve all your goals, as virtually all of the pleasure and excitement comes from working toward them. Miguel de Cervantes (1547–1616) expressed this well when he wrote: "The road is always better than the inn."

Allow miracles to enter your life, and enjoy your time on the road.

Notes

Introduction

1. Augustine of Hippo, *Epistle* 102. Many versions available, including: *Patrologiae cursus completus: series latina* (Edited by J. P. Migne, Paris, 1857–1866), 372.

2. St. Thomas Aquinas (translated by Vernon J. Bourke), *On the Truth of the Catholic Faith* (New York, NY: Doubleday and Company, 1956), ch. 102.

3. Pope Benedict XIV, *De Servorum Dei Beatificatione et Beatorum Canonizatione, iv De Miraculis* (Bologna, Italy, 1738), 1.1.12.

4. Paul Tillich, *Systematic Theology*, Volume 1 (London, UK: Nisbet, 1953), 130.

5. David Hume, *An Enquiry Concerning Human Understanding* (first published 1748. Second edition edited by L. A. Selby-Bigge, was published by the Oxford University Press in 1902), Section X: *Of Miracles*, page 211, footnote.

6. Richard Swinburne, *The Concept of Miracle* (London, UK: Macmillan and Company, 1970), 1.

7. C. S. Lewis, *Miracles: A Preliminary Study* (London, UK: Geoffrey Bles Limited, 1947), 15.

8. R. F. Holland, "The Miraculous," article in *American Philosophical Quarterly*, ii, (1965), 43. This article is reprinted in *Miracles*, edited by Richard Swinburne (New York, NY: Macmillan Publishing Company, 1989), 53–69.

9. George Woodcock, *The Crystal Spirit: A Study of George Orwell* (Boston, MA: Little, Brown and Company, 1966), 168.

10. John Evelyn, *Diary of John Evelyn*, Volume 3, edited by E. S. de Beer (1955), 96.

11. Richard Carew, quoted in William Camden, *Remains Concerning Britain* (London, UK, 1614), 224.

Chapter One

1. Willa Sibert Cather, *Death Comes for the Archbishop*, Book 1, Chapter 4. nd.

2. *Encyclopaedia Britannica, Micropaedia V* (Chicago, IL: Encyclopaedia Britannica, Inc., fifteenth edition, 1983), 322.

3. C. S. Lewis, *Miracles: A Preliminary Study*, 131–158.

4. Soren Kierkegaard, *Training in Christianity* (London, UK: Oxford University Press, 1941), 99.

5. Kenneth L. Woodward, *The Book of Miracles* (New York, NY: Simon and Schuster, Inc., 2000), 34.

6. Herbert Thurston, *The Physical Phenomena of Mysticism* (Chicago, IL: Henry Regnery Company, 1952), 174–175.

7. D. Scott Rogo, *Miracles: A Parascientific Inquiry into Wondrous Phenomena* (New York, NY: The Dial Press, 1982), 302–303.

8. Richard Webster, *Is Your Pet Psychic?* (St. Paul, MN: Llewellyn Publications, 2002), 122–123.

9. Eleanor Touhey Smith, *Psychic People* (New York, NY: William Morrow and Company, Inc., 1968), 13–20.

10. Carol Neiman, *Miracles: The Extraordinary, the Impossible, and the Divine* (New York, NY: Viking Studio Books, 1995), 80.

11. Montague Summers, *The Physical Phenomena of Mysticism* (London, UK: Rider and Company Limited, 1950), 123.

12. D. Scott Rogo, *Miracles: A Parascientific Inquiry into Wondrous Phenomena*, 82–83. nd.

13. Auguste Swerrens, *Blessed Saints* (Edinburgh, Scotland: Turner and Powers Limited, 1922), 147.

14. Karlis Osis and Erlendur Haraldsson, "OOBE's in Indian Swamis: Satya Sai Baba and Dadaji," article in *Research in Parapsychology*, 1975, edited by Joanna Morris, Robert Morris, and W. G. Roll. (Metuchen, NJ: Scarecrow Press, 1976).

15. Eric Dingwall, *Some Human Oddities* (New Hyde Park, NY: University Books, Inc, 1962), 88.

16. Stuart Gordon, *The Paranormal: An Illustrated Encyclopedia* (London, UK: Headline Book Publishing, 1992), 203.

17. Jocelyn Rhys, *The Reliquary: A Collection of Relics* (London, UK: Watts and Company, 1930), 2–4.

18. Ibid., 16.

19. Keith Thomas, *Religion and the Decline of Magic* (New York, NY: Charles Scribner's Sons, 1971), 26.

20. Harley Williams, *A Doctor Looks at Miracles* (London, UK: Anthony Blond Limited, 1959), 47–49.

21. *The British Daily Mail* reported on June 19, 1921 that "the peasants refuse to confess to any but the young friar or to receive Communion from another's hand, and in consequence the rest of the monastery is idle, while long queues besiege the young Franciscan and gaze in wonder at the markings on his hands, sandalled feet, and head."

22. Padre Pio, quoted in *The Friar of San Giovanni* by John McCaffery (London, UK: Darton, Longman and Todd, 1978), 3.

23. Oscar De Liso, *Padre Pio: The Priest Who Bears the Wounds of Christ* (New York, NY: McGraw Hill Book Company, 1960), 114–118.

24. Susy Smith, *Widespread Psychic Wonders* (New York, NY: Ace Publishing Corporation, 1970), 174–175.

25. Joseph E. Lifschutz, "Hysterical Stigmatization," article in *American Journal of Psychiatry*, 114, 1957, 527–531. Reprinted in *The Unfathomed Mind: A Handbook of Unusual Mental Phenomena* compiled by William R. Corliss (Glen Arm, MD: The Sourcebook Project, 1982), 683–688.

26. Joseph V. Klauder, "Stigmatization," article in *Archives of Dermatology and Syphology*, 37, 1938, 650–659. Reprinted in *The Unfathomed Mind: A Handbook of Unusual Mental Phenomena* compiled by William R. Corliss (Glen Arm, MD: The Sourcebook Project, 1982), 689–690.

27. Stuart Gordon, *The Book of Miracles: From Lazarus to Lourdes* (London, UK: Headline Book Publishing, PLC, 1996), 142–143.

28. Stuart Gordon, *The Paranormal: An Illustrated Encyclopedia* (London, UK: Headline Book Publishing, PLC, 1992), 229.

29. L. Zolondek, *Book XX of Al-Ghazali's Ihya' `Ulm Al-din* (Leiden, Netherlands: E. J. Brill, 1963). This list can also be found in *The Book of Miracles* by Kenneth L. Woodward (New York, NY: Simon and Schuster, Inc., 2000), 185–189.

30. There are many translations available of the Koran. Mine is The Qur'an, translated by Abdullah Yusuf Ali Elmhurst, NY: Tahrike Tarsile Qur'an, Inc.,2001). Sutra 17:88 says: "If the whole of mankind and Jinns were to gather together to produce the like of this Qur'an, they could not produce the like thereof, even if they backed up each other with help and support." Further evidence can be found in sutras 2:23 and 10:38.

31. The Qur'an, translated by Abdullah Yusuf Ali, Sutra 17:88. Sutra 6:109.

32. *Encyclopaedia Britannica, Macropaedia 12*, fifteenth edition (Chicago, IL: Encyclopaedia Britannica, Inc., 1983), 272.

33. Reginald A. Ray, *Buddhist Saints in India: A Study of Buddhist Values and Orientations* (New York, NY: Oxford University Press, 1994), 115.

34. Stephan Beyer, *Magic and Ritual in Tibet: The Cult of Tara* (New Delhi, India: Motilal Banarsidass Publishers Private Limited, 1988), 236. (Originally published by the University of California Press, Berkeley, CA, 1974).

35. *Shes-bya Magazine*, October 1968, 19. Reprinted in *Magic and Ritual in Tibet: The Cult of Tara* by Stephan Beyer, 240.

Chapter Two

1. Harley Williams, *A Doctor Looks at Miracles* (London, UK: Anthony Blond Limited, 1959), 55.

2. Claire Lesgretain, "Lourdes: What Makes a Miracle?" Article in *Miracles*, Volume 1, No. 1, (1994), 58.

3. Bernadette Soubirous, quoted in James Randi, *The Faith Healers* (Buffalo, NY: Prometheus Books, 1987), 22–23.

4. Terence Hines, *Pseudoscience and the Paranormal* (Buffalo, NY: Prometheus Books, 1988), 249.

5. Dr. Van Hoestenberghe, quoted in *The Invisible College* by Jacques Vallee (Chicago, IL: Henry Regnery Company, 1969), 159.

6. Jacques Vallee, *The Invisible College*, 162.

7. Edeltraud Fulda, *And I Shall Be Healed: The Autobiography of a Woman Miraculously Cured at Lourdes* (New York, NY: Simon and Schuster, Inc., 1961).

8. William Thomas Walsh, *Our Lady of Fatima* (New York, NY: Image Books, 1954), 69.

9. An English translation of his report can be found in *Our Lady of Fatima* by William Thomas Walsh, pages 147–148.

10. Heather Duncan, quoted in *A Walking Miracle* by Patricia Miller. Article in *Miracles*, Vol 1, Number 1 (1994), 48.

11. Dr. Andrija Puharich quoted in *The Romeo Error* by Lyall Watson (London, UK: Coronet Books, 1976), 212.

12. There are many accounts of Arigó's life, and the many healing miracles he performed. The most complete account is *Arigó—Surgeon of the Rusty Knife* by John G. Fuller (New York, NY: Thomas Y. Crowell Company, 1974).

13. Hudson Tuttle, *Studies in the Out-Lying Fields of Psychic Science* (New York, NY: M. L. Holbrook and Company, 1889), 174–175.

14. Brendan O'Regan, "Healing, Remission and Miracle Cures," in *Institute of Noetic Sciences Special Report* (May 1987), 3–14.

Chapter Three

1. P. D. Ouspensky, *Strange Life of Ivan Osokin* (London, UK: Faber and Faber Limited, 1948).

2. A. H. Z. Carr, *How to Attract Good Luck* (Hollywood, CA: Wilshire Book Company, 1965), 25–26.

3. Anonymous, "The Rise and Rise of a Rare Internet Success" (Article in *Sunday Star-Times*, Auckland, New Zealand, July 13, 2003), D11.

Chapter Four

1. Max Freedom Long, *Introduction to Huna* (Sedona, AZ: Esoteric Publications, 1975), 4. Originally published 1945.

2. Max Freedom Long, *The Secret Science Behind Miracles* (Marina del Rey, CA: DeVorss and Company, 1954), 14.

Chapter Five

1. Gina Cerminara, *Insights for the Age of Aquarius* (Wheaton, IL: Quest Books, 1973), 203–204.

2. Beverley Nichols, *Powers That Be: The X Force* (New York, NY: St. Martin's Press, 1966), 15.

3. Mrs. Anna Denton, quoted in *Encyclopaedia of Psychic Science* by Nandor Fodor (New Hyde Park, NY: University Books, Inc., 1966), 317. (Originally published by Arthurs Press, London, UK, 1933.) Mrs. Anna Denton Cridge was the sister of Professor William Denton who used psychometry to learn more about his geological specimens. He described his findings in three books: *Nature's Secrets* (Boston, MA: William Denton, 1863), *The Soul of Things: Psychometric Researches and Discoveries* (Boston, MA: Walker, Wise and

Company, 1863) and *Our Planet, its Past and Future* (Boston, MA: Denton Publishing Company, 1869).

4. Colin Wilson, *The Psychic Detectives* (London, UK: Pan Books, 1984), 30–31.

5. John M. Parker, "Suggestions Regarding Principles Acting in the Use of the Bantu Divining Basket," article in *Science*, 104, 1946, 513–514.

6. Richard Webster, *Omens, Oghams and Oracles* (St. Paul, MN: Llewellyn Publications, 1995), 38–39.

7. J. B. Rhine, "History of Experimental Studies," article in *Handbook of Parapsychology*, edited by Benjamin B. Wolman (New York, NY: Van Nostrand Reinhold Company, 1977), 32.

8. E. Douglas Dean, "Precognition and Retrocognition," article in *Psychic Exploration: A Challenge for Science* by Edgar D. Mitchell (New York, NY: G. P. Putnam's Sons, 1974), 160.

9. G. R. Price, "Science and the Supernatural," article in *Science*, August 26, 1966. See also G. R. Price, "Letter to the Editor," *Science*, January 28, 1972.

10. Helmut Schmidt, "Quantum Processes Predicted?" Article in *New Scientist*, 44, 1969, 114–115. Reprinted in *The Unfathomed Mind: A Handbook of Unusual Mental Phenomena* compiled by William R. Corliss, 223–224.

11. Critical responses to Dr. Schmidt's experiments can be found in: C. E. M. Hansel, *ESP and Parapsychology: A Critical Re-Evaluation* (revised edition). (Buffalo, NY: Prometheus

Books, 1980), Paul Kurtz (editor), *A Skeptic's Handbook of Parapsychology* (Buffalo, NY: Prometheus Books, 1985), and John L. Randall and others, Letter in *New Scientist*, 44, 1969, 259–260.

12. Stewart Robb, *Strange Prophecies That Came True* (New York, NY: Ace Books, Inc., 1967), 51.

13. Harry Houdini, *Miracle Mongers and Their Methods* (New York, NY: E.P. Dutton and Company, 1920), 84–87.

14. Arthur Osborn, *The Future is Now: The Significance of Precognition* (New Hyde Park, NJ: University Books, Inc., 1961), 87.

15. Winston Churchill, quoted in *My Darling Clementine* by Jack Fishman and W. H. Allen (London, UK: Pan Books, 1964), 136.

16. William Lilly, *Astrological Predictions* (New Delhi, India: Sagar Publications, 1962), 341. (Originally printed by Thomas Brudenell for John Partridge and Humphrey Blunden, London, UK, 1648.)

17. Colin Wilson, *Beyond the Occult* (London, UK: Bantam Press, 1988), 165.

18. Jeane Dixon, quoted in *The Story of Fulfilled Prophecy* by Justine Glass (London, UK: Cassell and Company, Limited, 1969), 185–186.

19. Justine Glass, *The Story of Fulfilled Prophecy*, 186.

20. Susy Smith, *Widespread Psychic Wonders* (New York, NY: Ace Publishing Corporation, 1970), 39.

21. J. C. Barker, "Premonitions of the Aberfan Disaster," article in *Journal of the Society for Psychical Research*, 44, 1967.

22. Louisa E. Rhine, *Hidden Channels of the Mind* (New York, NY: William Sloane Associates, 1961), 199.

23. W. E. Cox, "Precognition: An Analysis I and II," article in *Journal of the American Society for Psychic Research*, 50, 1956.

24. Brian Inglis, *The Paranormal: An Encyclopedia of Psychic Phenomena* (London, UK: Granada Publishing Limited, 1985), 69–70.

25. H. G. B. Erickstad, *The Prophecies of Nostradamus in Historical Sequence from AD 1550–2005* (New York, NY: Vantage Press, Inc., 1982), XIV.

26. There are many editions of Nostradamus' prophecies. The quatrains relating to Jack and Robert Kennedy are I:26, IV:14 and V:28. The quatrains relating to the Great Plague are IX:11 and II:53. Quatrain II:51 predicts the Great Fire of London.

27. Abraham Lincoln, quoted in *Recollections of Abraham Lincoln, 1847–1865* by Ward H. Lamon (Chicago, IL: McClurg and Company, 1937), 232.

28. Dorothy Armitage, *Dreams That Came True* (London, UK: Stanley Paul, Limited, 1942), 113–116.

29. J. W. Dunne, *An Experiment With Time* (London, UK: A. and C. Black Limited, 1927).

30. Miss Morison and Miss Lamont, *An Adventure*. First published 1911. I have the fourth edition, published by Faber and Faber Limited, London, UK, 1934.

31. Richard Webster, *The Complete Book of Palmistry* (St. Paul, MN: Llewellyn Publications, 2001), 43. Originally published 1994 as *Revealing Hands*.

Chapter Six

1. Aleister Crowley, *Magick Liber ABA* (Originally published 1913. Reprint, York Beach, ME: Samuel Weiser, Inc., 1994), 126.

2. Florence Farr, quoted in Mary K. Greer, *Women of the Golden Dawn: Rebels and Priestesses* (Rochester, VT: Park Street Press, 1995), 64.

3. Bishop Hugh Latimer, quoted in *Religion and the Decline of Magic* by Keith Thomas (New York, NY: Charles Scribner's Sons, 1971), 177.

4. Robert Burton, *Anatomy of Melancholy* (Originally published 1621. There are many editions available.), II, I, l.

5. Dion Fortune, *Psychic Self-Defense* (York Beach, ME: Samuel Weiser, Inc., 1992), 141–142.

6. There are many accounts of Jacques Aymar's search for the murderers. Good sources include: *Curious Myths of the Middle Ages* by the Rev. Sabine Baring-Gould (1869), *The Divining Rod* by Sir William Barrett and Theodore Bester-

man (1926), and *Dowsing for Beginners* by Richard Webster (St. Paul, MN: Llewellyn Publications, 1996).

Chapter Nine

1. Staff of *Reader's Digest, Into the Unknown* (Sydney, Australia: Reader's Digest Services Pty Ltd., 1982), 188–189.

2. Harvey Day, *Occult Illustrated Dictionary* (London, UK: Kaye and Ward Limited, 1975), 16.

3. Stuart Gordon, *The Paranormal: An Illustrated Encyclopedia*, 34.

4. Ruth Montgomery, *The World Before* (New York, NY: Coward, McCann and Geoghegan, Inc., 1976), xiii.

5. Rudyard Kipling, *Something of Myself: For My Friends Known and Unknown* (London, UK: Macmillan and Company, Limited, 1937), 146.

6. C. H. Broad, preface, *Swan on a Black Sea* by Geraldine Cummins (London, UK: Routledge and Kegan Paul, Limited, 1965), 7.

7. Jon Klimo, *Channeling* (Los Angeles, CA: Jeremy P. Tarcher, Inc., 1987), 80.

8. Patience Worth, quoted in *Patience Worth: A Psychic Mystery* by Casper S. Yost (London, UK: Skeffington and Son, Limited, 1916), 262.

9. Frederick Bligh Bond, *Glastonbury Scripts 1: The Return of Johannes* (London, UK: P. B. Beddow, 1921). The Glaston-

bury Scripts are a series of nine booklets edited by Frederick Bligh Bond. They record a series of automatic writings about Glastonbury Abbey from a number of sources. Bond kept his sources secret until his book, *The Gate of Remembrance* (Oxford, UK: Basil Blackwell, 1918), was published. This told the story of his many conversations with the long-dead monks at the abbey. Not surprisingly, this caused immense consternation with the church authorities. A co-director was appointed, and in 1922, Bond was dismissed and banned from the abbey grounds.

10. W. T. Stead, quoted in *The Unknown Guest* by Brian Inglis with Ruth West and the Koestler Foundation (London, UK: Chatto and Windus Limited, 1987), 196–197.

11. Stainton Moses, *Spirit-Identity* (London, UK: W. H. Harrison Limited, 1879), 38.

Chapter Ten

1. Aldous Huxley, *Island* (St. Albans, UK: Chatto and Windus Limited, 1962), 224.

2. Marc Barasch, "A Psychology of the Miraculous," article in *Psychology Today*, March/April 1994, 54–80.

3. Philip S. Haley, *Modern Loaves and Fishes—and Other Studies in Psychic Phenomena* (San Francisco, CA: P. S. Haley, 1935. Revised paperback edition 1960).

Suggested Reading

ʾAli, Muhammad. *The Religion of Islam*. United Arab Republic: National Publication and Printing House, n.d.

Beckworth, Francis J. *David Hume's Arguments Against Miracles: A Critical Analysis*. Lanham, MD: University Press of America, Inc., 1989.

Beyer, Stephan. *Magic and Ritual in Tibet: The Cult of Tara*. New Delhi, India: Motilal Banarsidass Publishers Private Limited, 1988. Originally published by the University of California Press, Berkeley, CA, 1974.

Boyd, Beverly. *The Middle English Miracles of the Virgin*. San Marino, CA: The Huntington Library, 1964.

Burns, R. M. *The Great Debate on Miracles: From Joseph Glanvill to David Hume*. Lewisburg: Bucknell University Press, 1981.

Carr, A. H. Z. *How to Attract Good Luck*. Hollywood, CA: Wilshire Book Company, 1965.

Corliss, William R. (compiler). *The Unfathomed Mind: A Handbook of Unusual Mental Phenomena*. Glen Arm, MD: The Sourcebook Project, 1982.

Dumont, Theron Q. *The Solar Plexus or Abdominal Brain*. n.d.

Ebon, Martin. *Prophecy in Our Time*. New York, NY: The New American Library, Inc., 1968.

Geisler, Norman L. *Miracles and Modern Thought*. Grand Rapids, MI: Zondervan Publishing House, 1982.

Glass, Justine. *The Story of Fulfilled Prophecy*. London, UK: Cassell and Company, Limited, 1969.

Gordon, Stuart. *The Book of Miracles: From Lazarus to Lourdes*. London, UK: Headline Book Publishing, 1996.

Grant, Robert M. *Miracle and Natural Law in Graeco-Roman and Early Christian Thought*. Amsterdam, Netherlands: North-Holland Publishing Company, 1952.

Houston, J. *Reported Miracles*. Cambridge, UK: Cambridge University Press, 1994.

Lawton, John Stewart. *Miracles and Revelation*. London, UK: Lutterworth Press, 1959.

Lewis, C. S. *Miracles: A Preliminary Study.* London, UK: Geoffrey Bles Limited, 1947.

Long, Max Freedom. *The Secret Science at Work: The Huna Method as a Way of Life.* Marina Del Rey, CA: DeVorss and Company, 1953.

————. *Growing Into Light.* Marina Del Rey, CA: DeVorss and Company, Inc., 1955.

————. *The Huna Code in Religions.* Marina Del Rey, CA: DeVorss and Company, Inc., 1965.

McCaffery, John. *The Friar of San Giovanni.* London, UK: Darton, Longman and Todd, 1978.

Miller, Carolyn. *Creating Miracles: Understanding the Experience of Divine Intervention.* Tiburon, CA: H. J. Kramer, Inc., 1995.

Mitchell, Edgar. *Psychic Exploration: A Challenge for Science.* New York, NY: G. P. Putnam's Sons, 1974.

Neiman, Carol. *Miracles: The Extraordinary, the Impossible, and the Divine.* New York, NY: Viking Studio Books, 1995.

Noble, Thomas F. X. and Thomas Head (editors). *Soldiers of Christ.* University Park, PA: The Pennsylvania State University Press, 1995.

Ray, Reginald A. *Buddhist Saints in India: A Study in Buddhist Values and Orientations.* New York, NY: Oxford University Press, 1994.

Rhys, Jocelyn. *The Reliquary: A Collection of Relics.* London, UK: Watts and Company, 1930.

Richo, David. *Unexpected Miracles: The Gift of Synchronicity and How to Open It.* New York, NY: The Crossroad Publishing Company, 1998.

Rogo, D. Scott. *Miracles: A Parascientific Inquiry into Wondrous Phenomena.* New York, NY: The Dial Press, 1982.

Schick, Theodore and Lewis Vaughn. *How to Think About Weird Things.* Mountain View, CA: Mayfield Publishing Company, 1995. Second edition 1999.

Shooman, A. P. *The Metaphysics of Religious Belief.* Aldershot, UK: Gower Publishing Company Limited, 1990.

Skafte, Dianne. *When Oracles Speak: Opening Yourself to Messages Found in Dreams, Signs, and the Voices of Nature.* London, UK: Thorsons, 1997.

Smith, Eleanor Touhey. *Psychic People.* New York, NY: William Morrow and Company, Inc., 1968.

Swinburne, Richard. *The Concept of Miracle.* London, UK: Macmillan and Company Limited, 1970.

Swinburne, Richard (editor). *Miracles*. New York, NY: Macmillan and Company, 1989.

Taylor, John. *Science and the Supernatural*. New York, NY: E. P. Dutton, 1980.

Van Dam, Raymond. *Saints and Their Miracles in Late Antique Gaul*. Princeton, NJ: Princeton University Press, 1993.

Ward, Benedicta. *Miracles and the Medieval Mind*. Philadelphia, PA: University of Pennsylvania Press, 1982.

Webster, Richard. *Omens, Oghams and Oracles*. St. Paul, MN: Llewellyn Publications, 1995.

————. *Seven Secrets to Success*. St. Paul, MN: Llewellyn Publications, 1997.

————. *Write Your Own Magic: The Hidden Power in Your Words*. St. Paul, MN: Llewellyn Publications, 2001.

Williams, Harley. *A Doctor Looks at Miracles*. London, UK: Anthony Blond Limited, 1959.

Wolman, Benjamin B. (editor). *Handbook of Parapsychology*. New York, NY: Van Nostrand Reinhold Company, 1977.

Zusne, Leonard and Warren H. Jones. *Anomalistic Psychology: A Study of Extraordinary Phenomena of Behavior and Experience*. Hillsdale, NJ: Lawrence Erlbaum Associates, Inc., 1982.

Index

☾ LLEWELLYN ORDERING INFORMATION

Order Online:
Visit our website at www.llewellyn.com, select your books, and order them on our secure server.

Order by Phone:
- Call toll-free within the U.S. at 1-877-NEW-WRLD (1-877-639-9753). Call toll-free within Canada at 1-866-NEW-WRLD (1-866-639-9753).
- We accept VISA, MasterCard, and American Express

Order by Mail:
Send the full price of your order (MN residents add 7% sales tax) in U.S. funds, plus postage & handling to:
Llewellyn Worldwide
P.O. Box 64383, Dept. 0-7387-0606-X
St. Paul, MN 55164-0383, U.S.A.

Postage & Handling:

Standard (U.S., Mexico, & Canada). If your order is:
Up to $25.00, add $3.50
$25.01 - $48.99, add $4.00
$49.00 and over, FREE STANDARD SHIPPING
(Continental U.S. orders ship UPS. AK, HI, PR, & P.O. Boxes ship USPS 1st class. Mex. & Can. ship PMB.)

International Orders:
Surface Mail: For orders of $20.00 or less, add $5 plus $1 per item ordered. For orders of $20.01 and over, add $6 plus $1 per item ordered.

Air Mail:
Books: Postage & Handling is equal to the total retail price of all books in the order.
Non-book items: Add $5 for each item.

Orders are processed within 2 business days.
Please allow for normal shipping time. Postage and handling rates subject to change.

Spirit Guides &
Angel Guardians
Contact Your Invisible Helpers

Richard Webster

They come to our aid when we least expect it, and they disappear as soon as their work is done. Invisible helpers are available to all of us; in fact, we all regularly receive messages from our guardian angels and spirit guides but usually fail to recognize them. This book will help you to realize when this occurs. And when you carry out the exercises provided, you will be able to communicate freely with both your guardian angels and spirit guides.

You will see your spiritual and personal growth take a huge leap forward as soon as you welcome your angels and guides into your life. This book contains numerous case studies that show how angels have touched the lives of others, just like yourself. Experience more fun, happiness, and fulfillment than ever before. Other people will also notice the difference as you become calmer, more relaxed, and more loving than ever before.

1-56718-795-1, 368 pp., 5³⁄₁₆ x 8 $9.95

Spanish edition
Ángeles guardianes y guías espirituales
1-56718-786-2, 336 pp., 5³⁄₁₆ x 8, illus. $12.95

Success Secrets
Letters to Matthew

Richard Webster

Matthew is lacking vision and passion in his life. His marriage is on the rocks and his boss is worried about Matthew's falling sales figures. Just as he is feeling the lowest he has felt in years, he goes to his mailbox and finds an envelope addressed to him, with no return address and no stamp. He instantly recognizes the handwriting as that of his old history teacher from high school. Wouldn't Mr. Nevin be dead by now? Why would Matthew get a letter from him after thirty years?

This little book is a quick read about following your dreams, setting goals, overcoming obstacles, pushing yourself even further, and making work fun.

> *Don't lead a half-life, Matthew. I'm trying to help you find your passion. When you find your passion you'll never work again. Of course, you'll probably work extremely hard, but it won't seem like work. And then, if you win millions of dollars, you'll carry on with whatever it is you are doing. Because it is your passion, your purpose, your reason for being here.*

1-56718-788-9, 168 pp., 5 ³⁄₁₆ x 8 $7.95

To order by phone, call 1-877-NEW-WRLD
Prices subject to change without notice

Soul Mates
*Understanding
Relationships Across Time*

Richard Webster

The eternal question: how do you find your soul mate—that special, magical person with whom you have spent many previous incarnations? Popular metaphysical author Richard Webster explores every aspect of the soul mate phenomenon in his newest release.

The incredible soul mate connection allows you and your partner to progress even further with your souls' growth and development with each incarnation. *Soul Mates* begins by explaining reincarnation, karma, and the soul, and prepares you to attract your soul mate to you. After reading examples of soul mates from the author's own practice, and famous soul mates from history, you will learn how to recall your past lives. In addition, you will gain valuable tips on how to strengthen your relationship so it grows stronger and better as time goes by.

1-56718-789-7, 216 pp., 6 x 9 $12.95

Spanish edition
Almas Gemelas
0-7387-0063-0, 216 pp., 5³⁄₁₆ x 8 $12.95

10 Spiritual Steps to a Magical Life
Meditations and Affirmations for Personal Growth and Happiness

Adrian Calabrese, Ph.D.

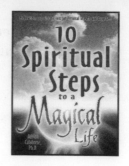

Awaken a new life in ten magical steps.

For a decade, Adrian Calabrese has helped others to unleash their spiritual power to achieve their greatest potential and create miracles in their lives. Now she outlines her simple approach that exceeds any religious dogma and offers the opportunity for unlimited spiritual growth.

You will learn how to tap into your extraordinary divine power to create a joyful, abundant life. When you follow the steps faithfully, you will begin to see your life change in a very special way. Not only will you become happier and more sensitive to others, you will notice that you suddenly attract whatever your heart desires!

0-7387-0311-7, 240 pp., 6 x 9, illus. $14.95

To order by phone, call 1-877-NEW-WRLD
Prices subject to change without notice

Discover Your
Spiritual Life
Illuminate Your Soul's Path

Elizabeth Owens

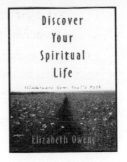

Some are led to the spiritual path by a mystical experience, by a tragic life circumstance, or by nagging feelings of discontent. Whatever the reason, you need a road map or guide to assist you along the way. Spiritualist medium Elizabeth Owens gives you the tools to connect with that higher guidance that, she says, already resides within yourself.

Learn a life-changing method for handling problems and disappointments. Discover effective ways to meditate, pray, create affirmations, forgive those who have hurt you, and practice gratitude. Process painful emotions and thoughts quickly through the art of becoming a balanced observer.

0-7387-0423-7, 264 pp., 5 ³/₁₆ x 8 $12.95

To order by phone, call 1-877-NEW-WRLD
Prices subject to change without notice

Lost Secrets of Prayer
Practices for Self-Awakening

Guy Finley

Do your prayers go unanswered? Or when they are answered, do the results bring you only temporary relief or happiness? If so, you may be surprised to learn that there are actually two kinds of prayer, and the kind that most of us practice is actually the least effective.

Best-selling author Guy Finley presents *The Lost Secrets of Prayer*, a guide to the second kind of prayer. The purpose of true prayer, as revealed in the powerful insights that make up this book, is not to appeal for what you think you want. Rather, it is to bring you to the point where you are no longer blocked from seeing that everything you need is already here. When you begin praying in this new way, you will discover a higher awareness of your present self. Use these age-old yet forgotten practices for self-awakening and your life will never be the same.

1-56718-276-3, 240 pp., 5 ¼ x 8 $9.95

Spanish edition
Los secretos perdidos de la oración
1-56718-281-x, 224 pp., 5 ³⁄₁₆ x 8 ¼ $7.95

To order by phone, call 1-877-NEW-WRLD
Prices subject to change without notice